Think Good, Feel Good

A Cognitive Behavioural Therapy Workbook for Children and Young People

Second Edition

Paul Stallard

WILEY

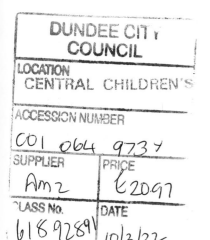
This edition first published 2019
© 2019 John Wiley & Sons Ltd

Edition History
John Wiley & Sons Ltd (2002)

All rights reserved. No part of this publication may be reproduced, stored in a retrieval system, or transmitted, in any form or by any means, electronic, mechanical, photocopying, recording or otherwise, except as permitted by law. Advice on how to obtain permission to reuse material from this title is available at http://www.wiley.com/go/permissions.

The right of Paul Stallard to be identified as the author of this work has been asserted in accordance with law.

Registered Offices
John Wiley & Sons, Inc., 111 River Street, Hoboken, NJ 07030, USA
John Wiley & Sons Ltd, The Atrium, Southern Gate, Chichester, West Sussex, PO19 8SQ, UK

Editorial Office
The Atrium, Southern Gate, Chichester, West Sussex, PO19 8SQ, UK

For details of our global editorial offices, customer services, and more information about Wiley products visit us at www.wiley.com.

Wiley also publishes its books in a variety of electronic formats and by print-on-demand. Some content that appears in standard print versions of this book may not be available in other formats.

Limit of Liability/Disclaimer of Warranty
While the publisher and authors have used their best efforts in preparing this work, they make no representations or warranties with respect to the accuracy or completeness of the contents of this work and specifically disclaim all warranties, including without limitation any implied warranties of merchantability or fitness for a particular purpose. No warranty may be created or extended by sales representatives, written sales materials or promotional statements for this work. The fact that an organization, website, or product is referred to in this work as a citation and/or potential source of further information does not mean that the publisher and authors endorse the information or services the organization, website, or product may provide or recommendations it may make. This work is sold with the understanding that the publisher is not engaged in rendering professional services. The advice and strategies contained herein may not be suitable for your situation. You should consult with a specialist where appropriate. Further, readers should be aware that websites listed in this work may have changed or disappeared between when this work was written and when it is read. Neither the publisher nor authors shall be liable for any loss of profit or any other commercial damages, including but not limited to special, incidental, consequential, or other damages.

Library of Congress Cataloging-in-Publication Data
Names: Stallard, Paul, 1955- author.
Title: Think good, feel good : a cognitive behavioural therapy workbook for
    children and young people / Paul Stallard, Professor of Child and Family
    Mental Health, University of Bath, UK and Head of Psychological Therapies
    (CAMHS), Oxford Health NHS Foundation Trust, UK.
Description: Second edition. | Hoboken, NJ : Wiley, 2019. | Includes
    bibliographical references and index. |
Identifiers: LCCN 2018023891 (print) | LCCN 2018024522 (ebook) | ISBN 9781119395317
    (Adobe PDF) | ISBN 9781119395300 (ePub) | ISBN 9781119395287 (paperback)
Subjects: LCSH: Behavior therapy for children. | Cognitive therapy for
    children. | Behavior therapy for teenagers. | Cognitive therapy for
    teenagers. | BISAC: PSYCHOLOGY / Clinical Psychology.
Classification: LCC RJ505.B4 (ebook) | LCC RJ505.B4 S72 2019 (print) | DDC
    618.92/89142–dc23
LC record available at https://lccn.loc.gov/2018023891

Cover Design: Wiley
Cover Image: © www.davethompsonillustration.com

Set in 10/13pt Legacy Sans by Thomson Digital, Noida, India
Printed and bound by CPI Group (UK) Ltd, Croydon CR0 4YY

C001121_271021

Think Good, Feel Good

Contents

About the author

Paul Stallard is Professor of Child and Family Mental Health at the University of Bath and Head of Psychological Therapies (CAMHS) for Oxford Health NHS Foundation Trust. He has worked with children and young people for almost 40 years since qualifying as a clinical psychologist in Birmingham in 1980.

Clinically, Paul continues to work within a specialist child mental health team where he leads a Cognitive Behaviour Therapy (CBT) clinic for children and young people with a range of emotional disorders including anxiety, depression, obsessive compulsive disorder (OCD), and post-traumatic stress disorder (PTSD).

He is an international expert in the development and use of CBT with children and young people and has provided training in many countries. He is an active researcher and has published widely many leading journals. Recent research projects have included large school-based CBT programmes for depression and anxiety and the use of eHealth with children and young people.

Acknowledgement

There are many people who have directly and indirectly contributed to the development of this book.

First, I would like to thank my family, Rosie, Luke, and Amy for their encouragement and enthusiasm. Despite many long hours working, writing, and travelling, their support for this project has been unwavering.

Second, I have had the good fortune to work with many amazing colleagues during my career. A number of our clinical discussions have informed the ideas in this book. Of my colleagues, I would particularly like to thank Kate and Lucy who I have had the privilege to work with in our CBT clinic for over a decade. Their patience, creativity, and thoughtfulness have helped me to develop and test the ideas contained in this book.

Third, I would like to thank the children and young people I have had the honour to meet. Their determination to overcome their challenges continues to inspire and motivate me to find ways in which effective psychological interventions can be made more available.

Finally, I would like to thank those who read this book. I hope that these materials will help you to help a young person make a real difference to their life.

Online resources

All the text and workbook resources in this book are **available free, in colour, to purchasers** of the print version. To find out how to access and download these flexible aids to working with your clients visit the website

www.wiley.com/go/thinkgoodfeelgood2e

The online facility provides an opportunity to download and print relevant sections of the workbook that can then be used in clinical sessions with young people. The materials can be used to structure or supplement clinical sessions or can be completed by the young person at home.

The online materials can be used flexibly and can be accessed and used as often as required.

CHAPTER ONE

Cognitive behaviour therapy: theoretical origins, rationale, and techniques

Cognitive behavioural therapy (CBT) is a generic term to describe psychotherapeutic interventions based on cognitive, behavioural, and problem-solving approaches. The overall aim of CBT is to facilitate an awareness of the important role of cognitions on emotions and behaviours (Hofmann, Sawyer, and Fang 2010). CBT therefore embraces the core elements of both cognitive and behavioural theories and has been defined by Kendall and Hollon (1979) as seeking to

> preserve the efficacy of behavioural techniques but within a less doctrinaire context that takes account of the child's cognitive interpretations and attributions about events.

CBT has established itself through numerous randomised controlled trials as an effective psychological treatment for children. It has proven to be effective in the treatment of anxiety (James et al. 2013; Reynolds et al. 2012; Fonagy et al. 2014), depression (Chorpita et al. 2011; Zhou et al. 2015; Thapar et al. 2012), post-traumatic stress disorder (Cary and McMillen, 2012; Gillies et al. 2013), chronic pain (Palermo et al. 2010; Fisher et al. 2014), and obsessive compulsive disorder (Franklin et al. 2015). In addition, CBT has informed many school-based prevention programmes and been found to be effective in reducing symptoms of depression (Hetrick et al. 2016; Calear and Christensen 2010), anxiety (Werner-Seidler et al. 2017; Stockings et al. 2016, Neil and Christensen 2009), and post-traumatic symptoms (Rolfsnes and Idsoe 2011).

The substantial body of knowledge demonstrating effectiveness has resulted in CBT being recommended by expert groups such as the UK National Institute for Health and Care Excellence (NICE) and the American Academy of Child and Adolescent Psychiatry for the treatment of young people with emotional disorders including depression, obsessive compulsive disorders, post-traumatic stress disorder, and anxiety. This growing evidence base has also prompted the development of a national training programme in the UK in CBT, Improving Access to Psychological Therapies (IAPT), which has now been extended to children and young people (Shafran et al. 2014).

> CBT is an evidence-based intervention for the prevention and treatment of psychological problems.

▶ The foundations of cognitive behaviour therapy

The theoretical basis for CBT has evolved over many years through the work of a number of significant influences. A review of this research is beyond the remit of this book, although it is important to note some of the key concepts and approaches that have underpinned and shaped CBT as we currently know it.

CBT is a generic term to describe therapeutic interventions based on behavioural, cognitive, and problem-solving approaches. It has evolved through three distinct phases or waves, each of which has significantly contributed to clinical practice.

▶ First wave: behaviour therapy

The first phase was based on learning theory and was shaped by the pioneering work of Pavlov (1927), Wolpe (1958), and Skinner (1974) demonstrating classical and operant conditioning. This work established how emotional responses, such as anxiety, could become associated (conditioned) with specific events and situations, i.e. spiders or talking with people. Thus anxiety could be reduced by pairing events that trigger the anxiety (i.e. seeing a spider, approaching a group of people) with an antagonistic response (relaxation). This procedure (systematic desensitisation) continues to be widely used in clinical practice and involves graded exposure, both in vivo and in imagination, to a hierarchy of feared situations whilst remaining relaxed.

The second major influence of behaviour therapy highlighted the important role of environmental influences on behaviour. This work demonstrated that behaviour is triggered by environmental influences (antecedents) and that the consequences which follow will influence the likelihood of that behaviour occurring again. Behaviour will increase in occurrence if it is followed by positive consequences (positive reinforcement), or not followed by negative consequences (negative reinforcement). A detailed understanding of antecedents and the use of reinforcement to increase adaptive behaviours continue to be widely used techniques in CBT interventions.

> Relaxation training, systematic desensitisation, exposure, and reinforcement are effective techniques.

▶ Second wave: cognitive therapy

The second phase built on the efficacy of behavioural techniques by paying attention to the personal meanings and interpretations that individuals make about the events that occur. This was heavily influence by the work of Ellis (1962), Beck (1976), and Beck et al. (1979) who proposed that problems with emotions and behaviour arise from the way events are construed rather than by the event per se. As such, emotions and behaviours can be changed by challenging the meanings and ways in which events are processed. This led to the development of a comprehensive understanding of different types of cognitions (core beliefs, assumptions, and automatic thoughts); their focus (cognitive triad – about me, the future, the world); their content (personal threat, failure, responsibility, and blame); and the way in which information is processed (selective and biased). This is summarised in Figure 1.1.

In terms of cognitions, the strongest and deepest are core beliefs (or schemas) which are developed during childhood as a result of significant and/or repeated experiences. Overly critical and demanding parents may, for example, lead a child to develop a belief that they are a 'failure'. Core beliefs are very strong, global, rigid, fixed ways of thinking that are resistant to change. They underpin the meanings and interpretations that we make about ourselves, our world, and our future and lead us to make predictions about what will happen. The child with a belief that they are a 'failure' will therefore expect to fail in most situations.

These beliefs are activated by events similar to those that produced them (i.e. school tests). Once activated, attention, memory, and interpretation processing biases filter and select information that is

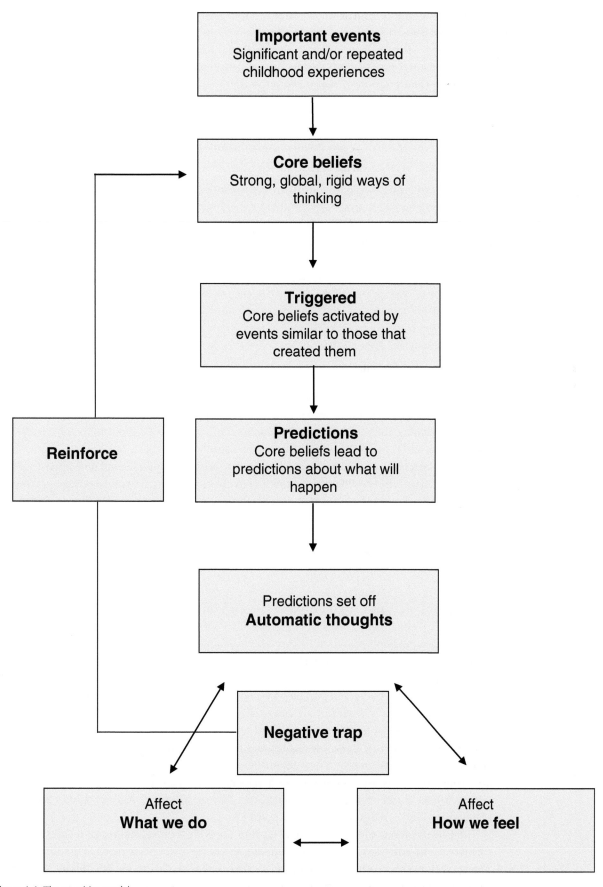

Figure 1.1 The cognitive model.

consistent with the belief. Attention biases result in attention being focused on information that confirms the belief (i.e. looking for evidence of failure), whilst neutral or contradictory information is overlooked. Memory biases result in the recall of information that is consistent with the belief (i.e. remembering past failures), whilst interpretation biases serve to minimise any inconsistent information (find a reason to negate any success).

> Identifying and challenging attention, memory, and interpretation processing biases can improve psychological functioning

The most accessible level of cognitions are automatic thoughts or 'self-talk'. These are the constant stream of thoughts that race through our minds providing a running commentary about what we do. These are related to our core beliefs with dysfunctional and negative beliefs producing negative automatic thoughts. A child with a belief that they are a failure may experience a stream of negative automatic thoughts such as 'I will get this wrong', 'I can't do this', and 'what is the point of trying when I never do well' when preparing for a school test.

The focus of cognitive therapy is on the content and nature of the processing deficits and biases that are underpinning the child's problems. In general, young people who are anxious tend to have cognitions and biases towards the future and personal threat, danger, vulnerability, and inability to cope (Schniering and Rapee 2004; Muris and Field 2008). Depression tends to be related to cognitions concerning loss, deprivation, and personal failure with the process of rumination increasing feelings of hopelessness (Kendall, Stark, and Adam 1990; Leitenberg, Yost, and Carroll-Wilson 1986; Rehm and Carter 1990). Aggressive children tend to perceive more aggressive intent in ambiguous situations, selectively attend to fewer cues when making decisions about the intent of another person's behaviour, and generate fewer verbal solutions to problems (Dodge 1985; Lochman, White, and Wayland 1991; Perry, Perry, and Rasmussen 1986).

Interventions involve the identification of biased or selective cognitions and processing (negative thinking, thinking errors) which are then subject to objective testing (cognitive evaluation). Testing involves challenging selective attention biases by attending to overlooked information; challenging memory biases by recalling contradictory experiences, and challenging interpretation biases by exploring alternative explanations. This leads to the final stage (cognitive restructuring) where more functional and balanced thoughts, assumptions, and beliefs are developed.

▶ Third wave: acceptance, compassion, and mindfulness

Cognitive therapies have proven to be very effective, although there remains a minority of people who do not respond to this form of psychotherapy. Some do not find the process of actively challenging and re-appraising specific cognitions easy or acceptable. Similarly, a number of studies have highlighted that changes in cognitions are not necessarily related to improved emotional well-being. Changes occur without directly and explicitly challenging the content of cognitions.

This has led to what has been called a third wave of cognitive behaviour therapies (Hofmann, Sawyer, and Fang 2010). These psychotherapies focus on changing the nature of the relationship between the individual and their own internal events rather than actively changing the content of their cognitions. This has been led to the development of Acceptance and Commitment Therapy (Hayes 2004; Hayes et al. 2006), Compassion-Focused Therapy (Gilbert 2009, 2014) and Mindfulness (Segal, Williams, and Teasdale 2012).

These interventions encourage the individual to live with, tolerate, and accept their experiences, cognitions, and emotions rather than attempting to change them. This requires the individual to connect with and experience the here and now with openness and curiosity. Mindfulness techniques are used to increase awareness as attention is focused on internal and external events as they occur.

Thoughts and emotions are accepted without judgement as ongoing internal mental events and physiological reactions that are separate from their personal core identity.

A second theme is that of acceptance where individuals learn to accept and value themselves for who they are rather than constantly criticising themselves for their imperfections or weaknesses. This value-based approach helps the individual to focus on those aspects of life which are personally important and motivates them to work towards their goals.

The third theme is that of compassion where self-criticism is replaced with self-kindness. Individuals are helped to focus on their strengths, positive skills, and acts of kindness. Compassionate reasoning helps to develop balanced, kinder, alternative thinking where self-criticism is replaced with self-compassion. Compassionate behaviour encourages the individual to behave in more helpful ways such as facing frightening events or displaying self-kindness. Compassionate imagery helps to create a positive self-image, whilst compassionate feeling helps to notice and experience acts of kindness from others.

> Our relationship with our thoughts and feelings can be changed by mindfulness, acceptance, and self-compassion

▶ Core characteristics of cognitive behaviour therapy

Although CBT is used to describe a range of different interventions, they often share a number of core features.

CBT is theoretically determined

CBT is based upon empirically testable models. Strong theoretical models provide the rationale for CBT, i.e. cognitions are associated with emotional problems and inform the content of the intervention, i.e. change the nature of the cognitions or our relationship with them. CBT therefore provides a cohesive and rational intervention and is not simply a collection of disparate techniques.

CBT is based on a collaborative model

A key feature of CBT is the collaborative process by which it occurs. The child has an active role in identifying their goals, setting targets, experimenting, practicing, and monitoring their performance. The approach is designed to facilitate greater and more effective self-control, with the therapist providing a supportive framework within which this can occur. The role of the therapist is to develop a partnership in which the child is empowered to develop a better understanding of their problems and to discover alternative ways of thinking and behaving.

CBT is time limited

It is often brief and usually time limited, consisting of no more than 16 sessions, and in many cases far fewer. The brief nature of the intervention promotes independence and encourages self-help. This model is readily applicable to work with children and adolescents, for whom the typical period of intervention is considerably shorter than that with adults.

CBT is objective and structured

It is a structured and objective approach that guides the young person through a process of assessment, problem formulation, intervention, monitoring, and evaluation. The goals and targets of the intervention are explicitly defined and regularly reviewed. There is an emphasis on quantification and the use of ratings (e.g. the frequency of inappropriate behaviour, strength of belief in thoughts, degree of distress experienced, or progress towards achieving goals). Regular monitoring and review provides an objective way of assessing progress by comparing current performance against baseline assessments.

CBT has a here-and-now focus

CBT interventions focus upon the present, dealing with current problems and difficulties. They do not seek to 'uncover unconscious early trauma or biological, neurological, and genetic contributions to psychological dysfunction, but instead strives to build a new, more adaptive way to process the world' (Kendall and Panichelli-Mindel 1995). This approach has high face validity for children and young people, who may be more interested in and motivated to address real time, here-and-now issues, rather than understanding their origins.

CBT is based on a process of guided self-discovery and experimentation

It is an active process that encourages self-questioning and the development and practice of new skills. Children are not simply passive recipients of therapist advice or observations, but are encouraged to observe and learn through a process of experimentation. The link between thoughts and feelings is investigated and alternative ways of changing the content or nature of the relationship with his or her thoughts is explored.

CBT is a skills-based approach

CBT provides a practical, skills-based approach to learning alternative patterns of thinking and behaviour. Children are encouraged to practice skills and ideas that are discussed during therapy sessions in their everyday life, with home practice tasks being a core element of many programmes. These provide opportunities to identify what is helpful and how potential problems can be resolved.

CBT is theoretically determined.

It is based on a model of active collaboration.

It is brief and time limited.

It is objective and structured.

It focuses on current problems.

It encourages self-discovery and experimentation.

It advocates a skills-based learning approach

▶ The goal of cognitive behaviour therapy

The overall aim of CBT is to improve current well-being and to enhance resilience and future coping. This is achieved through developing increased self-awareness, improved self-control, and enhancing personal efficacy through the promotion of helpful cognitive and behavioural skills. The process of CBT moves the young person from a dysfunctional to a more functional cycle as illustrated below.

Dysfunctional cycle

Thoughts
Overly negative
Self-critical and judgemental
Selective and biased

Behaviour
Avoid
Give up
Inappropriate
Unhelpful

Feelings
Unpleasant
Anxious
Depressed
Angry
Out of control

Functional cycle

Thoughts
More positive and balanced
Acknowledge success & strengths
Accepting and non-judgemental

Behaviour
Confront
Try
Appropriate
Helpful

Feelings
Pleasant
Relaxed
Happy
Calm
In control

CBT helps to reduce the negative effect of what people think (cognitions) on how they feel (emotions), and what they do (behaviour). This is achieved by either actively focusing on the content of the child's cognitions or by changing the nature of their relationship with them.

- If *focusing on content*, the child is encouraged to observe and identify common dysfunctional thoughts and beliefs that are predominantly negative, biased, and self-critical. Through a process of self-monitoring, education, and experimentation, these are tested and replaced by more balanced and functional cognitions that acknowledge strengths and success.

- If *focusing on the relationship* with cognitions, the child is encouraged to stand back from his or her thoughts and to observe them in a curious, non-judgemental way as passing cognitive activity. Mindfulness maintains attention on the here and now with the young person being encouraged to accept themselves and the events that occur.

The core components of cognitive behaviour therapy

CBT includes a range of techniques and strategies that can be used in different sequences and permutations. This flexibility allows interventions to be tailored towards particular problems and the individual needs of the child rather than being delivered in a standardised cookbook approach. Similarly, the wealth of techniques means that CBT can be used for prevention to enhance future coping and resilience as well as an intervention to reduce current psychological distress.

Although the primary focus of second wave (i.e. test and challenge the content of cognitions and processes) and third wave (i.e. change the nature of the relationship with our thoughts) CBT differ, embedded within these approaches are a number of different skills and techniques.

Psycho-education

A basic component of all cognitive behavioural programmes involves education about the link *between thoughts, feelings, and behaviour*. The process involves developing a clear and shared understanding of the relationship between how people think, how they feel, and what they do. In addition, the collaborative process of CBT and the *active role* of practice and *experimentation* are stressed.

Values, goals, and targets

CBT may involve identifying important *personal values*. These help to maintain focus on the future and act as a framework for motivating and guiding behaviour towards their achievement.

Goal setting is an inherent part of all cognitive behaviour programmes. The *overall goals* of therapy are mutually agreed and defined in ways that can be objectively assessed. The transfer of skills from therapy sessions to everyday life is encouraged by the systematic use of *assignment tasks* where new skills are practiced in real-life settings. Progress towards the achievement of *specific targets* is regularly reviewed and provides an objective way of assessing change.

Acceptance and acknowledgement of strengths

CBT helps the individual to recognise and acknowledge their *strengths and achievements*. Personal strengths can be empowering and can be used to cope with future challenges and problems. *Acceptance* is also emphasised so that rather than constantly trying to change things which are beyond his/her control events, emotions and thoughts are accepted for what they are.

Thought monitoring

The key task of developing a better understanding of common cognitions is achieved through observing and monitoring cognitions and patterns of thinking. Thought monitoring could focus on the specific content of *core beliefs, negative automatic thoughts, or predictions* to identify those that produce strong emotional reactions or are overly negative or self-critical. Alternatively, *observation* could be encouraged whereby the young person is helped to develop an awareness of the effect of their cognitions on their emotions.

Identification of cognitive distortions and deficits

The process of thought monitoring provides an opportunity to identify common *negative or unhelpful cognitions, beliefs or predictions*. In turn, this results in increased awareness of the nature and type of *cognitive distortions* (e.g. magnification, focusing on the negative), *cognitive deficits* (e.g. misinterpretation of others cues as negative, limited range of problem-solving skills), and the effect of these upon mood and behaviour.

Thought evaluation and developing alternative cognitive processes

The identification of dysfunctional cognitive processes leads to the systematic *testing and evaluating of these predictions and beliefs* and the learning of alternative cognitive skills. The development of a process of *balanced thinking* or *cognitive restructuring* is encouraged. This may involve a process of looking for new information, thinking from another person's perspective, or looking for contradictory evidence, which may result in dysfunctional cognitions being revised.

The evaluation provides an opportunity to develop alternative, *more balanced, and functional* cognitions, which recognise difficulties but acknowledge strengths and success.

Development of new cognitive skills

CBT involves the development of new cognitive skills such as *distraction* where attention is focused away from anxiety-increasing stimuli towards more neutral tasks. Cognitive coping can be enhanced through the use of *positive self-talk* with *consequential thinking and problem-solving skills* helping to develop alternative ways of thinking through challenges.

Mindfulness

CBT may develop new cognitive skills such as *mindfulness* where attention is focused non-judgementally on the present moment. Rather than reacting to, or attempting to change what we think or how we feel, mindfulness helps to develop curious observation and acceptance of our internal processes. This here-and-now focus reduces negative cognitive rehearsal of future events and rumination about past events.

Affective education

Many programmes involve emotional education designed to *identify and distinguish core emotions* such as anger, anxiety, or unhappiness. Programmes may focus upon the *physiological changes* associated with these emotions (e.g. dry mouth, sweaty hands, and increased heart rate) in order to facilitate a greater awareness of the child's unique expression of each core emotion.

Affective monitoring

The monitoring of strong or dominant emotions can help identify *times, places, activities, or thoughts* that are associated with both pleasant and unpleasant feelings. *Scales* are used to rate the intensity of emotion both during real-life situations and treatment sessions and provide an objective way of monitoring performance and assessing change.

Affective management

New emotional management skills are developed to help *tolerate distress* and/or manage emotions more effectively. This may involve techniques such as *progressive muscle relaxation, controlled breathing, calming imagery, self-soothing,* or *distraction.*

Greater awareness of the individual's unique emotional pattern can lead to the development of *preventative strategies.* An awareness of the anger build up may, for example, enable a child to stop his/her emotional progression at an earlier stage thereby preventing an aggressive outburst. Similarly the adoption of *kindness and compassion* throughout everyday life can help to develop a greater acceptance of what occurs and so prevent problems occurring.

Activity monitoring

This can be used to promote awareness of the link between *what we do and how we feel and behave.* This helps to develop a better understanding of how some activities or events are associated with different feelings and ways of thinking.

Behaviour activation

Activity monitoring can lead to *behavioural activation* whereby the individual is encouraged to become more active. This may involve *increasing activities* that create enjoyment, involve others, produce a sense of achievement, or encourage physical activity. Being active can have a positive effect upon mood.

Activity rescheduling

Engagement in activities that create more pleasant emotions can also be encouraged by *activity rescheduling.* This involves rescheduling positive mood-lifting activities to occur on those days or at those times that are currently associated with strong unpleasant emotions.

Skills development

A structured *problem-solving* process can provide a useful framework for confronting and dealing with challenges rather than putting decisions off or avoiding them. A number of CBT interventions also focus on the development of *interpersonal effectiveness* by enhancing skills such as conflict resolution, assertiveness, and developing and maintaining friendships.

Behavioural experiments

CBT is based upon a process of guided discovery during which predictions and thoughts are challenged and tested. A powerful way to undertake this is to objectively check things out by setting up *behavioural experiments*. These can help to test whether predictions and thoughts are always right, to discover alternative explanations for events or, what might happen if things were done differently.

Fear hierarchy and exposure

A core aim of CBT programmes is to encourage children to face and learn to cope with challenging situations or events. This can be achieved through a process of *graduated exposure* where problems are defined, the overall task broken into smaller steps and then each is ranked in a hierarchy of ascending difficulty. Starting with the least difficult, the child is exposed to each step of the *hierarchy*, either in vivo or imagination. Once successfully completed, they move to the next step, progressing through the hierarchy until the problem has been mastered.

Role play, modelling, exposure, and rehearsal

The learning of new skills and behaviours can be achieved in a variety of ways. *Role play* provides an opportunity to practice dealing with difficult or challenging situations such as coping with teasing. Role play enables positive skills to be identified and alternative solutions or new skills highlighted. A process of *skills enhancement* can facilitate the process of acquiring new skills and behaviours. Observing others *model appropriate behaviour* or skills can then result in new behaviour being *rehearsed* in imagination before being *practiced in real life* through *exposure* tasks.

Self-reinforcement and reward

A cornerstone of all CBT programmes is *positive reinforcement* and acknowledgement of effort. We need to care for ourselves and to value what we do. This could take the form of *self-reinforcement*, for example, cognitively (e.g. 'Well done, I coped well with that situation'), materially (e.g. downloading a special song), or by activities (e.g. special relaxing bath). Reinforcement should be based on effort and attempting to do things rather than upon the achievement of a successful outcome.

CBT provides the clinician with a rich toolbox of techniques that can be used flexibly to meet the needs and interests of the child. These are summarised in the Clinician's Toolbox (Figure 1.2).

CBT programmes includes a mix of the following:

Psycho-education

Identification of values, goals, and strengths.

Monitoring of thoughts, feelings, and/or behaviour.

Acceptance of what cannot be changed.

Identification, challenging, or observation of cognitions.

Developing new cognitive skills.

Learning alternative ways to manage unpleasant emotions.
Learning new behaviours.

Target-setting and home-based practice.

Positive reinforcement.

Psycho-education
Understand the link between thoughts, feelings, and behaviour

Values, goals, and targets
Identify personal values, agree, goals and targets

Acceptance and acknowledgement of strengths
Recognise positives and strengths and accept who you are

Cognitions

Thought monitoring
Negative automatic thoughts
Core beliefs/schema
Dysfunctional assumptions

Identification of cognitive distortions and deficits
Common dysfunctional cognitions, assumptions, and beliefs
Patterns of cognitive distortions
Cognitive deficits

Thought evaluation
Testing and evaluating cognitions
Cognitive restructuring
Development of alternative, balanced thinking

Development of new cognitive skills
Distraction, positive and coping self-talk, self-instructional,
consequential thinking

Mindfulness
Curious and non-judgemental observation

Behaviour ——————————————— Emotions

Activity monitoring
Link activity, thoughts and feelings

Behavioural activation
Increase mood lifting activity

Activity rescheduling
Timetable activities

Skills development
Problem-solving and interpersonal effectiveness

Behavioural experiments
Test predictions/assumptions
Discover new meanings

Fear hierarchy and exposure
Face challenges in a graded way

Affective education
Distinguish between core emotions
Identify physiological bodily symptoms

Affective monitoring
Link feelings with thoughts and behaviour
Scales to rate intensity

Affective management
Relaxation, self-soothing, mind games,
imagery, controlled breathing

Self-reinforcement
Take care of yourself and reward yourself

Figure 1.2 The clinicians toolbox.

Cognitive behaviour therapy with children and young people

▶ Cognitive behaviour therapy with children

Cognitive behavioural therapy (CBT) can involve a complex set of skills to systematically identify, test, and challenge cognitions and processes. Similarly, an ability to 'think about thinking' is involved in those approaches that require the child to observe, acknowledge, and accept cognitions and emotions. These processes involve a degree of cognitive maturity and sophistication and require an ability to engage in abstract tasks such as viewing events from different perspectives, generating alternative attributions or standing back, and curiously observing thoughts and emotions. The degree to which young children have the required level of cognitive maturity to be able to engage in such tasks has been the subject of debate.

Developmental research suggests that very young children understand that people have internal mental states such as thoughts, beliefs, and images that may represent or, misrepresent, the world (Wellman, Hollander, and Schult 1996). Three-year-old children understand that thought bubbles represent what a person may think, can distinguish between thoughts and actions, understand that people can have different thoughts about the same event, and that thoughts can misrepresent an event. Flavell, Flavell, and Green (2001) suggest that by the age of five children are able to articulate their cognitions and understand the concept of self-talk, a common strategy in many CBT programmes. Similarly, children aged four to seven are able to distinguish between thoughts, feelings, and behaviours (Quakley, Reynolds, and Coker 2004) and that children as young as five years could generate post-event attributions, name emotions, and link thoughts and feelings (Doherr et al. 2005). This has led some reviewers to conclude that 'young children (aged 5–8) can demonstrate the cognitive capacity to benefit from creatively delivered forms of CBT' (Grave and Blissett 2004).

A few trials evaluating the effectiveness of an adapted form of CBT with young children have now been reported. CBT-based interventions have been found to be effective with anxious children as young as five years (Monga, Young, and Owens 2009), four years (Hirshfeld-Becker et al. 2010), and three years of age (Klaus Minde et al. 2010). A trauma-focused CBT-based intervention was found to be effective with children aged three to six (Scheeringa et al. 2011) and an adapted CBT intervention for children aged five to eight with obsessional compulsive disorder (Freeman et al. 2008). This supports the widely held clinical view that children aged seven and above can readily engage in some form of adapted CBT.

Children aged seven years can readily engage in CBT.

Think Good, Feel Good: A Cognitive Behavioural Therapy Workbook for Children and Young People, Second Edition. Paul Stallard.
© 2019 John Wiley & Sons Ltd. Published 2019 by John Wiley & Sons Ltd.
Companion website: www.wiley.com/go/thinkgoodfeelgood2e

Although CBT can be sophisticated and complex, many of the tasks require an ability to reason effectively about concrete matters and issues rather than abstract conceptual thinking (Harrington, Wood, and Verduyn 1998). The concrete operational stage of cognitive development typically acquired during the middle years (7–12 years of age) is sufficient for many of the basic tasks of CBT (Verduyn 2000). CBT should be fun, interesting, and engaging, with materials and concepts presented at an age-appropriate level (Young and Brown 1996).

Concrete and familiar examples

Familiar images and examples can provide concrete ways of helping children to understand some of the ideas and concepts of CBT.

Freeman et al. (2008) described the rationale for exposure as 'taking a medicine that tastes "yucky" but makes you feel better'. Obsessional thoughts can be described as 'having a song stuck in your head'. The image of a tumble drier can be used to explain how thoughts get locked in our heads and keep tumbling round and round. A CD playing in the child's head can be used to describe repetitive automatic thoughts, whilst Barrett, Webster, and Turner (2000) suggested that automatic thoughts can be visualised as 'thought invaders'. Similarly, a DVD player can be used to explain repetitive intrusive images.

Concrete examples such as these can lead to the development of self-control strategies. The child can be encouraged to imagine turning off his/her CD or DVD or to spot and destroy their thought invaders. A pair of negative glasses can be used to describe the common cognitive distortion of selective abstraction where only negative things are noticed. The child can be encouraged to change their glasses and to look again for any positive things that they overlooked.

Play

Younger child will typically feel more comfortable with play-based activities rather than verbal discussions. Ronen (1992) described how the concepts of automatic thoughts (i.e. 'doing something without thinking about it') and mediated thoughts (i.e. 'a command or order that the brain sends to the body') were conveyed through a game of soldiers with the commander (brain) sending orders to their soldiers (your body). Similarly, automatic thoughts were explained whilst painting a river, where the river could either wander wherever it choose (automatic thoughts) or the flow could be changed and made to go where the child wanted (mediated thoughts).

Barrett, Webster, and Turner (2000) described how children were taught problem-solving through a fun task requiring them to move a balloon, without touching it, from one side of a room to another. Sorting games can be used to help children distinguish between thoughts, feelings, and actions. Quizzes provide a useful and entertaining way of accessing children's cognitions or helping them to develop skills such as distinguishing between helpful and unhelpful thoughts. Role plays provide engaging ways to rehearse and practice coping skills and activities such as creating a TV advert can be used to encourage children to reflect upon what they have learned.

Exposure tasks are core elements of CBT programmes for anxiety and can be adapted in playful ways. Hirshfeld-Becker et al. (2008), for example, encouraged children with separation anxiety to engage in a treasure hunt where they had to leave their parent to find the treasure. Similarly, young people with social anxiety can be encouraged to approach others in order to conduct surveys.

With young children, dolls and puppets can be used to assess and explore potentially important cognitions and to develop coping skills. Situations that the child finds difficult can be acted out with the puppets and the child invited to suggest what each puppet may be thinking or feeling. Similarly, the child can be encouraged to coach the puppet through difficult situations thereby providing an opportunity to develop and practice coping skills.

Metaphors

Metaphors are a useful way of describing abstract concepts in familiar terms (Friedberg and Wilt 2010). A good metaphor should be simple, concrete, and relate to objects or events that the child is familiar with (Killick, Curry, and Myles 2016). A common and familiar metaphor which can be used with young children and adolescents is the traffic light. From an early age children learn that the red light means 'stop', amber is to 'get ready', and green means 'go'.

This simple and familiar metaphor can be used in many ways. First, it can help children understand that there are different ways of thinking. Some ways of thinking are unhelpful (red thoughts) because they 'stop' them from doing things or make them feel uncomfortable. Other ways of thinking are more helpful (green thoughts) because they encourage the child 'to go' and do the things they would like to do or which make them feel better.

The traffic light sequence provides a simple three-step process to develop alternative more helpful (green) thoughts. At the red light, the child is encouraged to 'stop' and to catch the red thoughts that are tumbling around their head. At amber, the child is asked to 'get ready' and to identify alternative, more helpful, positive, and coping ways of thinking. At the green light, the child is encouraged to 'go' and to use their new (green) thoughts to test whether these are more or less helpful.

The traffic light can also be used as a way of developing a simple three-step problem-solving approach. Red means 'stop' and define the problem. Amber means 'get ready' and to find and explore alternative solutions. Green is 'to go' and to choose a solution and to see what happens.

A volcano provides a concrete way of visualising anger. The child can be helped to plot the stages as his/her anger builds. This can be used to help the child find ways to intervene at an early stage to stop the volcano from blowing its top.

Automatic thoughts can be conceptualised as computer spam or 'pop-ups' and the metaphor developed to help the adolescent develop a more robust firewall. Similarly, familiar terms can be used to define cognitive distortions. Thus rather than using complicated and abstract language such as catastrophisation or negative anticipation, terms such as *disaster thinking* or *fortune telling* can be used.

Imagery

The use of imagery has been reported with children as young as five years of age. Positive coping images can be used as a way to facilitate a strong positive affect, which is antagonistic to unpleasant emotional reactions such as anxiety or anger. Jackson and King (1981) used the image of the comic character Batman to help a young boy overcome his fear of the dark. Similarly, imagery could be used with older children where, for example, a comic image like a person wearing a silly hat might help to diffuse angry feelings arising from teasing. In order to be effective, positive coping images need to be tailored to the age of the child and be built upon his/her existing interests and fantasies (Rosenstiel and Scott 1977). In this respect, the Harry Potter books and films which are popular with children provide a rich source of material. When the character Ron Weasley was, for example, confronted with his fear of a giant spider, he beat his fear by confronting it whilst creating an image of the spider being funny.

Calming imagery can also be useful where the child is helped to create a multi-sensory image of a real or imaginal place that they find relaxing. A picture or drawing can help to visualise the image in detail which is then strengthened by attending to any sounds, smells, tastes, and tactile sensations.

Stories and workbooks

There are a number of useful storybooks that can be used as an adjunct to CBT. These help children understand their problems and symptoms and highlight some of the ways they can learn to overcome them. A full review of these is beyond the remit of this book, but the following provide some examples. The Huge Bag of Worries (Ironside and Rodgers 2011) is a story for children under the age of 11 that helps them to recognise that worries grow and grow unless they are confronted. The School

Wobblies (Wever 1999) has a number of engaging cartoons that will appeal to older children. It describes the sort of worries children have that prevent them from going to school and some of the tricks that can be used to beat them. *The Secret Problem*, also by Chris Wever (2000), is presented in a similar style. It focuses upon obsessive-compulsive disorders (OCD) and shows how compulsive behaviours can be chased away. Finally, *the Panic Book* (Phillips 1999) uses fun cartoons and words to describe panic disorders and how worrying situations need to be challenged and faced rather than avoided.

There are also many engaging stories and workbooks for younger children. For example, *Starving the Anger Gremlin* provides fun activities to help children understand why they become angry and to control their angry feelings to make the Anger Gremlin go away (Donnelly 2012). There is a similar workbook to help with anxiety (Donnelly 2013). *A Nifflenoo Called Nevermind* is a story about bottling up expressing, while *Draw on your Emotions* provides many practical exercises to help children express how they feel (Sunderland 1997, 2001). Finally, there are many workbooks that have been developed for children to convey the ideas of CBT in fun and engaging ways (Friedberg and McClure 2015; Barrett 2004).

Non-verbal materials

CBT with children needs to be delivered in an interesting and engaging way and will require a mix of verbal and non-verbal techniques. A range of materials will be useful, and it is helpful to ensure that visual media such as black/white boards, flip charts, drawing materials, and work sheets are available. Indeed, the use of visual stimuli such as cartoons and drawings can enhance young children's understanding of their symptoms and feelings (Scheeringa et al. 2011).

For those who are not verbally forthcoming, more visual activities involving cartoons, thought bubbles, and quizzes can be helpful. Worksheets involving simple pictures/cartoons with thought bubbles over the characters' head can be used to help children understand that a thought bubble can be used to represents what a person is thinking. Multiple thought bubbles introduce the child to a core concept of CBT namely that of alternative thinking, i.e. there is more than one way of thinking about the same event. Unfinished sentences can be used to identify thoughts related to specific situations and feelings (Friedberg and McClure 2015).

Visual materials are also helpful with older children. Diagrams summarising case formulations can be very powerful and empowering. Printed handouts can provide useful adjuncts to clinical sessions and provide a written record of key issues for future reference. Similarly, pies charts can provide an objective way of identifying, quantifying, and challenging assumptions about the likelihood of events occurring. Finally, visual rating scales are useful to promote and encourage a wider range of dimensionality thereby challenging the categorical thinking that is often common with children.

Clear steps and processes

For children, the process of cognitive restructuring in which dysfunctional cognitions are identified, tested, and reappraised can prove challenging (Spence, Donovan, and Brechman-Toussaint 2000). However, the process can be simplified into a simple set of steps which define the key processes involved. This can be very helpful even if the child is unable to recognise overarching rules, the cognitive processes they use, or generalise their conclusions to other situations.

A specific step process such as the 4Cs ('catch it, check it, challenge it, change it') provides a simple way to remember the process of thought identification, evaluation, and reappraisal. The child is therefore taught to notice when they feel unpleasant and to catch what they are thinking. Once identified, the thought is checked to see whether they have fallen into a thinking trap (biased ways of thinking). The next step is to challenge their thoughts by looking to see whether they have overlooked anything positive and important. The process ends by asking the child to reflect on this new information and to change the thought to something that is more helpful.

Alternatively, the young person can put their thoughts on trial and to look for the evidence to support and question them (de Oliveiraa et al. 2015). The process involves identifying the culprit (unhelpful way of thinking) and looking for evidence to support this way of thinking (the defence). The next stage is to look for evidence that would question this way of thinking (the prosecution). Witnesses, such as the young person's best friend or family, are invited to provide their view on the unhelpful thoughts culminating in a way of thinking that better fits the facts (the verdict).

Processes such as this can be made more appealing through the use of metaphors encouraging children to assume the role of a 'Private I' (Friedberg and McClure 2015) or 'thought tracker' (Stallard 2002) as they endeavour to catch their unhelpful thoughts.

Technology

Older children are highly familiar with, and competent in, using computers, the Internet, and smartphones. Technologies such as these are very appealing and offer a way of engaging with this age group (Boydell et al. 2014).

Laptop computers and smartphones may offer a more engaging way of completing diaries. The transportability of these devices can help the quick and accurate recording of mood, thoughts, or positive events as they occur. They can provide a way for children to 'download their heads' when they notice any 'hot thoughts' or strong emotional reactions. Because young people are often texting and interacting with mobile devices briefly recording information such as this will not attract peer attention.

Smartphone cameras provide older children with a way of recording difficult or challenging situations. Images can be reviewed to check some of the child's thoughts or assumptions about what is happening and can help plan how to cope with difficult situations. The child's photo-library can include pictures of their calming place which can remind and help them to create their image when required. Similarly, the child can load positive coping statements or reminders about processes such as thought challenging (e.g. 4Cs) on to their home page to prompt them to challenge their thoughts.

The Internet provides a helpful way of researching and normalising common problems such as feeling anxious or low in mood. Celebrities who have suffered such conditions can be found and ways in which these celebrities learned to succeed identified as possible options for the child to consider. Websites which provide guidance and instructions on techniques such as mindfulness or relaxation can be accessed to facilitate and guide practice. Similarly, there is a wealth of useful videos of young people talking about their personal experiences of psychological problems and strategies they found helpful. Learning from others can be very powerful with video stories and YouTube clips providing helpful ways to do this.

> To make CBT engaging and accessible, use age-appropriate methods to match the concepts and ideas of CBT to the developmental level and interests of the child.

▶ Facilitating engagement in CBT

In order to engage in CBT, children need to be able to

- access and communicate their thoughts
- generate alternative attributions about events
- identify and understand different emotions
- link thoughts, feelings, and situations

Although these skills are not necessarily prerequisites for engaging in CBT, the potential for these to develop during the course of the intervention should be evident.

Accessing and communicating thoughts

■ Direct questioning: describe what you are thinking

Interviewing can provide a rich source of information about the child's thoughts and self-talk. It has been suggested that, during an interview, children as young as three years of age can provide information about their thoughts (Hughes 1988).

At the simplest level, this can be determined by asking a child to describe 'what you are thinking' or 'what thoughts were running through your head'. Some children will be able to identify and articulate a range of thoughts relating to the cognitive triad. They may report thoughts relating to the perception of themselves (e.g. 'I feel silly talking with you'; 'You must think I'm an idiot to get upset by these things'), of the world as unfair (e.g. 'I had to miss football training to come here'; 'It's my mum who has got the problem. Talk with her not me'.) or the future (e.g. I don't think there is any point me being here. It's not going to make any difference').

However, a number of children will respond to such direct questioning with comments such as 'I don't know' or 'I wasn't thinking about anything'. This does not necessarily imply that the child cannot access his or her thoughts, but rather suggests the need to try an alternative, indirect approach.

■ Indirect approaches: describe a recent difficult situation

Younger children will probably find it easier to talk about a recent difficult situation. Help them to describe it, or draw a picture about it, and as they talk or draw, note whether the child is able to provide both a description of what happened and some of their thoughts/attributions about what occurred. Prompting the child for their thoughts at specific times, such as prior to, during, or immediately after an event can provide a useful structure for helping to identify their 'self-talk' (Kendall and Chansky 1991). At other times, careful probing and prompting during the interview may help the child to gain access to their thoughts, as illustrated in the example below.

Gill (9) becomes very upset when her mother goes out. There was a recent incident when her mother was going out for the evening where Gill panicked resulting in her mother cancelling her arrangements and staying at home. The discussion with Gill went as follows:

CLINICIAN:	It sounds as if you were really upset when mum was getting ready to go out. Can you tell me what happened, Gill?
GILL:	Mum was going out with her friends. I didn't want her to go out. As she put on her coat, I started to feel really bad.
CLINICIAN:	You felt really bad?
GILL:	Yes. Really frightened. My heart raced, and I felt really hot.
CLINICIAN:	What happened next?
GILL:	I started to cry and asked mum to stay with me.
CLINICIAN:	What did mum do?
GILL:	She told me there was nothing to worry about and that she would see me in the morning.
CLINICIAN:	How did that make you feel?
GILL:	It made me feel even worse. If mum really cared, she would have stayed at home with me.
CLINICIAN:	What happened next?
GILL:	Mum got really angry. She said I always play up when she wants to go out.

CLINICIAN:	Is that what happens?
GILL:	No, I don't play up. I just worry about her and want to make sure she is OK.
CLINICIAN:	Is mum ill?
GILL:	I think she is OK. I know she takes tablets for something.
CLINICIAN:	So what might happen if she goes out with her friends?
GILL:	I don't know. She could become ill and get taken to hospital, and I wouldn't know where she is.

The clinician provided Gill with a series of very concrete questions ('what', 'how', 'is' questions) which require a factual or descriptive response. 'Why' questions are harder to answer and often shut down conversations rather than those that require a descriptive response.

This very brief discussion showed that Gill was able to access and share her thoughts. Gill was worried that her mother would become ill and would not return home. When she goes out, Gill panics, and her mother stays at home where Gill can make sure she is safe.

■ What might someone else be thinking?

Younger children may have difficulty accessing and describing their own cognitions, but may be able to take a third-party perspective (Kane and Kendall 1989). As previously mentioned, younger children can use puppets and games to create and role play difficult situations. In the course of play, the child can be asked to show or say what the puppets might be thinking. At other times, simply taking the focus off the child and engaging in a conversation about what someone else might think in that situation might be helpful.

■ Thought bubbles

An alternative non-verbal approach is to provide the child with cartoons or pictures and to ask them to suggest what the people/characters may be thinking. This approach has been advocated by Kendall and Chansky (1991) and has been used in the Coping Cat programme for treating anxiety (Kendall 1992). In Coping Cat the child is, for example, asked to suggest what an ice skater or a child cooking a sausage on a BBQ might be thinking.

This approach can be simply adapted by the clinician depending upon the materials they have available. A child could, for example, suggest what the cat and goldfish maybe thinking in this picture.

gollykim/istock via Getty Images

Generating alternative attributions

A second core task of CBT is to help children learn that there are different ways of thinking about the same event. Children often become fixed on the idea that there is only one way of thinking.

Helping them to generate alternative thoughts begins the process of questioning their current way of thinking.

■ Hypothetical situations

Doherr, Corner, and Evans (1999) devised a series of simple hypothetical situations to assess whether children are able to identify alternative attributions for events. The child is presented with a series of scenarios, some of which are modelled on, and adapted from, those used by Greenberger and Padesky (1995). By way of an example, 'a child in a playground shouts "hello" at his friend, but his friend just runs past'. The child is then asked to think of as many different explanations as he/she can for what has happened.

Approaches such as this can also be used to explore problem-solving skills. A child can be presented with a pictorial vignettes and be asked to generate as many solutions as possible.

■ Generative cartoons

The child can be given a series of pictures or cartoons and then be asked to draw or write as many ideas as he/she can about what the character may be thinking. This can help the child to recognise that there are many different ways of thinking about the same event and begins the process of identifying helpful and unhelpful ways of thinking. In the picture below the child can be asked to complete the thought bubbles by drawing or writing what the dog might be thinking about his homework.

Illustration Works/Alamy Stock Photo

Awareness of emotions

A core element of many CBT programmes is affective education designed to help children become aware of and distinguish between different feelings. In order to participate in such a process, children need to be able to access their feelings and provide a description of them.

There are many different materials available to help children identify and express their own emotions through play, games, and drawing. Young children may not necessarily be able to provide a verbal description of their feelings, but they may be able to draw them. Similarly, they may only talk about one feeling such as being angry, although on careful questioning, it might emerge that there is an 'angry angry', a 'sad angry', or a 'scared angry'.

Quizzes and games can be used to assess whether the child can identify the feelings of another person. Children can be given pictures of people in different emotional states and asked to identify what they might be feeling from a list of emotions. Similarly, the clinician could role play different emotions and ask the child to suggest a name for each feeling.

Thoughts, feelings, and events

The theoretical model that underpins CBT is based on the connection between thoughts, feelings, and behaviours. Very simply, some ways of thinking are unhelpful (red thoughts) because they make the child feel unpleasant and stop them from doing things. Other ways of thinking are more helpful (green thoughts), make the child feel pleasant and encourage them to try.

Once again, the use of puzzles and quizzes will allow you to determine whether the child is able to demonstrate an awareness of different emotions in different situations. For example, the child could be provided with or generate a set of feeling cards (e.g. frightened, happy, and angry) and be asked to place the card that best describes how they feel with various situations (e.g. first day at school, playing with my best friend, or being told off). Similarly, the task could involve matching feelings with a range of different thoughts (e.g. 'I think I am going to get this wrong'; 'I think I played well in this game'; or 'I think my friends will tease me').

To engage in CBT, children need to

- Access and communicate their thoughts
- Generate alternative attributions about events
- Be aware of different emotions
- Link thoughts, feelings and situations

▶ Common problems when undertaking CBT with children

Limited verbal skills

The process of CBT with young children is typically less didactic than that with adults. Children may adopt a more passive, listening role during sessions. Whilst this may require greater input from the clinician, it does not necessarily imply that the child is unable to engage in CBT. As previously highlighted, the clinician needs to be flexible in their approach and to adjust the materials to match the child's interests and preferences. In these situations, a greater use of non-verbal materials is helpful, and children will often vocalise their thoughts and feelings whilst playing or drawing. Similarly the use of media such as whiteboards and flip charts can attract the child's interest and result in increased participation.

At other times, despite the creative use of materials, children may remain silent throughout sessions and respond with vague, non-committal answers to any probes or questions. On these occasions, it might be helpful to employ a more rhetorical approach whereby you guess aloud what the child might reply to questions. Similarly, if the child is reluctant to talk about him or herself, then discussing the similar problems of a third party, or acting them out through the use of puppets or play, can often result in more engagement. Finally, it may be useful to change the setting, so rather than sitting in the clinic, try going for a drink or a walk and see if the child becomes more communicative in a more relaxed environment.

Limited cognitive skills

A basic level of cognitive, memory, and verbal skills is required to engage in CBT, and consequently children with significant developmental issues may not be able to directly engage in the process. However, it needs to be established whether this is due to the child's limited cognitive abilities or to cognitive tasks not being pitched at the right level to allow the child to access them.

Presenting information more visually, using simpler language, and presenting abstract concepts in more concrete ways can make it easier for people with learning disabilities to engage in CBT

(Whitaker 2001). Memory problems can be overcome by the use of visual cues and prompts. For example, a child who is learning to use traffic lights as a way of problem-solving (red, stop and think; amber, plan; green, try it out) can be reminded to use the system at school by wrapping coloured strips around their pen. Similarly, tasks can be simplified with fewer decision points so that a child could be helped to 'bail out' (i.e. walk away from) situations in which they might lose their temper, rather than learning a more complex set of responses.

Difficulty accessing thoughts

Children often find it difficult to identify and vocalise their thoughts, particularly in response to direct questions. However, careful listening will reveal that beliefs, assumptions, and appraisals are often evident as they talk. At these times, it is often useful for the clinician to adopt the role of the 'thought catcher' described by Turk (1998) where the clinician identifies important cognitions when they occur and, at an appropriate time, brings them to the attention of the child. The clinician may stop the dialogue and bring the child's attention to the cognitions they have just verbalised, or alternatively, they may be held and summarised at a suitable time. For example, the clinician may listen to a child's description of a recent 'hot' situation and then summarise the key feelings and associated thoughts that they identified.

Children often confuse thoughts and feelings, leading Belsher and Wilkes (1994) to highlight the need to 'chase the effect'. The authors suggest that during clinical sessions particular attention should be paid to changes in emotion, which are feedback to the child in order to identify the associated cognitions (e.g. 'You seem to be thinking about something that is making you angry'). Often, children will require further help to discover their cognitions, and the clinician can either pursue Socratic questioning or provide a list of possible suggestions which the child can reject or agree with. By a process of observation and careful questioning, the child can discover and vocalise the cognitions underlying their emotions.

Lack of engagement

Children do not usually refer themselves for psychological help. They are usually brought to the clinician by concerned carers and professionals. The children themselves may not share these concerns or indeed perceive any particular problems that require help.

A core feature of CBT is the collaborative nature of the intervention, and if the child is unable to identify any goals or changes they would like to make, then the use of CBT or indeed any other psychotherapeutic approach should be questioned. However, this requires careful exploration, since the child's inability to identify possible goals may be a result of his or her experience (i.e. 'this is the way it has always been and always will be'). Helping the child to explore alternative, realistic possibilities may help him/her to recognise that his/her situation could be different. Similarly, a lack of motivation, as found, for example, with depressed children, may result in the expression of reluctance and hopelessness. In these instances, motivational interviewing maybe helpful in securing the young person's commitment to at least experimenting with CBT (Miller and Rollnick 1991). Motivational interviewing utilises basic counselling techniques (e.g. empathy, positive regard, and active listening) and cognitive behavioural interventions (e.g. positive restructuring, reinforcement) to increase a person's commitment to change. During this process, the child is encouraged to express his or her own views and perceptions of events whilst the clinician selectively listens for and reinforces possible sign of motivation.

No responsibility for securing change

Children may identify difficulties and targets for change, but may not view themselves as responsible for achieving them. Sometimes, this will be appropriate, but at other times, difficulties may be attributed to organic factors (e.g. 'This is me, I was born like this') or external factors that are not perceived as being within the individual's ability to change. For example, a child who is regularly in trouble at school may attribute this externally as being unfairly picked on by teachers (e.g. 'If the teachers didn't pick on me, then I wouldn't be in trouble'). Whether this is really the case, or whether it is a reflection of distorted or biased views, needs to be assessed. However, the child needs to be open-minded and prepared at least to explore his/her personal contribution to these events.

Involving parents

When working with children, it is important to consider how to involve parents and what their role in the intervention might be (Stallard 2005). Parents can be involved in a very limited way by, for example, attending the end of each of session or 1 or 2 joint review meetings with their child (e.g. parents involved as a cofacilitator). Parents could also be more actively involved in their child's treatment by attending each session with their child. The focus remains on the child's problems, whilst ensuring that parents are fully aware of the skills their child is acquiring so that they can prompt and encourage their use (e.g. parents involved as a cotherapist). Alternatively, CBT involves both child- and parent-focused sessions. For example, children could be helped to develop and practice skills to deal with anxiety, whilst parents learn news ways of encouraging and rewarding their child for facing their worries (e.g. parent involved as a co-client).

There is no conclusive evidence to suggest that parents must be involved in CBT programmes with their children or what is the best way to involve them (Breinholst et al. 2012). School-based CBT programmes to prevent anxiety, for example, have been found to be effective without any parental involvement (Stallard et al. 2014). At other times, it may be apparent that parents are trying too hard to protect their child from their problems in a way that has become unhelpful. Joining in with their child's habits and routines to prevent them becoming upset, for example, does not help the child discover that their habits are unnecessary. Involving parents in sessions with their child would provide an opportunity for parents to understand the effect of their behaviour on their child's routines and to explore alternative ways of responding.

On other occasions parents might have their own psychological problems which might dominate meetings. A parent and a child might, for example, be involved in the same traumatic event. However, the parent's distress might be overwhelming and prevent the child being able to openly discuss their own cognitions or emotions. In this instance, the child's needs would probably not be addressed if their parents were involved in every session. The decision about how and when to involve parents needs to be made on a case-by-case basis.

Collaboration with the parent or child?

A more fundamental issue arising from the involvement of parents relates to the process of collaboration and whether the child or their parent is seen as the primary client. This can be a source of tension, since children may identify different goals and targets to their parents, raising the question of whose agenda should be addressed. Pursuing the parent's or adult's agenda raises ethical issues with regard to whether their goals are coercive, designed to secure conformity or really concerned with furthering the best interests of the child.

The clinician needs to manage these different perspectives by listening and expressing interest in each whilst maintaining a detached, objective, and impartial position. Repeatedly clarifying and re-ferring back to the overall goal of therapy, namely to reduce the child's psychological distress, helps to maintain the focus, whilst highlighting that this goal can often be achieved in a number of ways. For example, a child who is anxious and unable to attend school might suggest an initial goal of going out with friends. Feeling more comfortable with friends could provide them with additional support as they return to school. Parents may advocate a more direct approach preferring to set goals about school attendance. Initially, responding to the child's agenda conveys a strong message to the child that his/her views are important and that they have a key role in determining change. However, the parent's goals are not lost or forgotten but are parked and returned to once the initial goals have been achieved.

To maximise early success, goals should be clear and achievable. The acronym SMART is a way of ensuring that goals are Specific, Measurable, Achievable, Relevant, and Timely. A good goal should be clearly and positively defined (specific) and which can be readily assessed (measured) to determine progress. The target should be motivating but not too large to feel impossible (achievable). Goals should be important to the young person (relevant) and be achievable within a reasonable timeframe (timely). Regularly reviewing progress provides an opportunity to monitor change, reassess the goals of the child, and his/her parents and identify and agree on the next target.

On other occasions, the child and their parents can be helped by the clinician to agree on a common focus. The protocol for treating OCD developed by March, Mulle, and Herbel (1994) provides an example of how the child and his/her parents can work together to overcome the child's obsessions. The child is encouraged to give his or her OCD a nasty name and to learn how to boss back obsessional urges. The parents are helped to distinguish between OCD and their child by externalising OCD as an illness that they can help their child overcome. The parents and their child work together as a team to beat OCD.

Significant family dysfunction

The dynamics within a family are complex and can result in individual children being inappropriately perceived as responsible for all of the family's difficulties. In such situations, individual CBT would not be appropriate if it did not address the wider family issues. Similarly, if the child's perceived cognitive deficits or distortions reflect limited parental capabilities or maladaptive parental views, then individual CBT would be inappropriate and unlikely to be effective. The clinician needs to undertake a thorough assessment in order to determine whether the child's comments that his/her parents are 'always putting me down' represent a cognitive distortion or an accurate reflection of a dysfunctional family. Determining this will indicate whether individual CBT or a more systemic approach is indicated.

Failure to undertake home-based assignments

CBT is an active process that typically involves the gathering of information and the practice of skills outside of clinical sessions. Although some children are interested and keen to undertake home-based assignments, others are unwilling to do so and repeatedly fail to complete tasks. This issue needs to be discussed openly with the child, the rationale and importance of the assignments explained, and the extent of what can realistically be undertaken, if anything, agreed. Terminology is important, and it is useful to avoid calling out-of-session assignments or experiments 'homework', which may be viewed negatively by the child.

Identifying an appropriate way of undertaking the task is also important. For example, children may be reluctant to write a thought diary but may be more interested in keeping a record on their computer or phone. Similarly, some children may be more motivated to email their thoughts to you, whilst others may prefer to 'download their head' into a voice recorder.

Completing home-based assignments is not a prerequisite for undertaking CBT. The experiences, thoughts, and feelings of children who are unable to keep records can still be assessed during clinical sessions. They can be asked to talk you through a recent difficult situation, and the clinician can probe and explore the thoughts and feelings that accompanied the event.

However, home-based assignments become more important during the skill development and consolidation phase. This is where the child practices skills under everyday conditions to discover those that are helpful. Without practice, the child will not be able to effectively transfer their skills into their everyday life and learn to behave in different ways. However, as the intervention progresses, it is anticipated that the therapeutic relationship will strengthen and become more open and honest thereby facilitating discussions about how home-based assignments can be made easier.

Brief interventions

Children often adopt a short-term problem-focused perspective. They are typically interested in addressing immediate pressing problems which are happening 'here and now'. Consequently, with children there is greater emphasis on facilitating and developing cognitive coping skills rather than addressing schemas or beliefs. Typically, there is less focus on abstract complexities, such as understanding the subtle nuances of different types of cognitive distortions. Instead, children are often keen to understand their difficulties within a cognitive framework and to learn more appropriate cognitive and behavioural skills to enable them to cope with them. This predominant focus on real-time problems often results in CBT with children being undertaken in relatively few clinical sessions. Although a number of structured CBT interventions for children identify 12–16 session programmes, clinical experience suggests that many interventions are considerably shorter than this. Important and significant change can be achieved in six or even fewer sessions.

'I get it, but I don't believe it'

There will be times when children understand the aims and methods of CBT but appear to go through the process in an academic and detached way. Thoughts may be systematically challenged and alternatives developed, but the child simply does not believe what they have discovered. Similarly, they might understand the aim of accepting and non-judgementally observing thoughts but are unable to stop arguing and engaging with them. Whilst there may be a need for further explanation and practice, it may become apparent that this approach does not work with this child.

In the true spirit of partnership, this needs to be acknowledged and openly discussed. Whilst a guiding principle of CBT is for the child to discover what works for them, it is equally important to discover what does not help. Potential barriers need to be explored and the option of changing from a thought-challenging approach to one of observing and accepting (or vice versa) discussed. If the alternative is still not acceptable to the child, then an alternative non-CBT approach should be considered.

> Common problems encountered when undertaking CBT with children include the following:
>
> - Limited verbal or cognitive skills and difficulty accessing thoughts.
> - Lack of engagement and/or problem ownership.
> - Identifying the role of parents and how to involve them.
> - Significant family dysfunction.
> - Failure to undertake home-based assignments.
> - Rapid change or problems understanding the approach.

CHAPTER THREE

Think good, feel good: an overview of materials

Think Good, Feel Good is a collection of materials that have adapted the concepts and strategies of cognitive behavioural therapy (CBT) for use with children and adolescents. Through three main characters, the Thought Tracker, Feeling Finder, and Go-Getter, children and young people are helped to understand the cognitive behavioural framework, to explore their cognitions, and to learn alternative cognitive and behavioural skills. The characters may be of more interest to younger children, who may find it easier to think about and describe thoughts and feelings through a third party. For older children, it maybe appropriate to focus more upon the materials and concentrate less upon the characters.

Think Good, Feel Good is not intended to be delivered systematically as a package. It does not represent a standardised course, nor is it a comprehensive CBT programme. Instead, it provides a range of materials that can be used flexibly depending upon the needs of the child and the nature of their difficulties. The materials provide examples of how the concepts of CBT can be conveyed in an enjoyable, simple, and understandable way.

Think Good, Feel Good provides educational materials and accompanying exercises for each of the following topics:

1. accept and be kind to yourself

2. be mindful

3. the link between thoughts, feelings, and behaviour

4. automatic thoughts

5. common thinking traps

6. challenging thoughts and balanced thinking

7. core beliefs

8. developing new cognitive skills

9. identifying feelings

10. strategies for controlling unpleasant feelings

11. ideas for changing behaviour

12. approaches to problem-solving

Each topic has an explanatory section that provides a concrete and understandable summary of the key issues. Illustrations and practical examples provide a way of relating the materials to issues and problems with which the child may find familiar. The explanatory section can be

Think Good, Feel Good: A Cognitive Behavioural Therapy Workbook for Children and Young People, Second Edition. Paul Stallard.
© 2019 John Wiley & Sons Ltd. Published 2019 by John Wiley & Sons Ltd.
Companion website: www.wiley.com/go/thinkgoodfeelgood2e

photocopied and used as a handout, or can be used to structure the session. The clinician can then emphasise and focus on those issues that are most relevant for the child.

A series of worksheets accompany each section to help the child apply the information to his or her own particular difficulties. The worksheets provide examples of how the concepts can be conveyed and are intended to be used flexibly and to be adapted by the clinician.

▶ Be kind to yourself

Summary

This section focuses on the need for acceptance and the development of a kind and compassionate approach to everyday life. This draws on ideas from the third wave of CBT and develops skills to promote health and well-being. Through these, children learn to accept themselves for who they are rather than criticising and finding fault with themselves and what they do. They are also helped to develop a kind and compassionate approach rather than being harsh and critical of themselves.

- Accept yourself for who are you are.
- Recognise your strengths.
- Be kind to yourself.

Worksheets

This section introduces the child to eight ways that they can be kinder to themselves. We are often very critical of ourselves but would never say these sorts of things to our friends. *Treat yourself like a friend* helps the child to catch their critical inner voice and to think about what they would say to a friend if they heard them saying these sort of things. Rather than constantly criticising and finding fault with themselves, *accept who I am* helps the child to identify their strengths and special qualities. To counter the tendency to go over events and beat themselves, *care for yourself* encourages the child to look after themselves and to find ways to help them feel better. *A kinder inner voice* is designed to help the child speak to themselves in a kinder way. They are encouraged to practice saying aloud short statements which acknowledge how they are feeling, that they are not the only ones to feel like this, and that they need to be kind to themselves. Finally, *finding kindness* helps the child to look for and notice the kind things that they or others do.

▶ Here and now

Summary

This section draws on ideas from mindfulness to help the child focus on what is happening here and now. Much time is spent rehearsing the negative things that happen or worrying about things going wrong. Focusing on what is happening here and now can help the child to clear the clutter that is tumbling around in their head.

This child is introduced to mindfulness through five steps captured by the acronym FOCUS. This involves focusing attention (F) and observing (O) what is happening here and now in a curious way (C). Children are encouraged to use (U) their senses to maximise the experience and to stay (S) with it, gently bringing their attention back when it wanders.

- Focus attention on what is happening.
- Observe what is happening.
- Curious approach.
- Use your senses.
- Stay with it.

Worksheets

Instructions are provided for a range of exercises to help the child integrate mindfulness into their everyday life. *FOCUS on your breathing* is a quick exercise that can be done anywhere that helps the child to focus on their breathing. Similarly, *FOCUS on your eating* is a short exercise that can be done at mealtimes which encourages the child to focus on what they are eating. *FOCUS on an object* is an activity that can completed once a day to help child focus on everyday objects we often take for granted. *Make a clutter jar* is a way of visualising the thoughts that tumble around our heads and how they will settle. *Thought spotting* encourages the child to step back from their thoughts and not to engage or argue with them. This theme is continued in *let feelings float away* where the child is encouraged to step back from their feelings and to watch them come and go.

▷ Thoughts, feelings, and what you do

Summary

This section provides an introduction to CBT and explains the link between thoughts, feelings, and behaviour. Different types of thoughts (automatic and core beliefs) are explained, the role of our predictions is highlighted, and the effects of helpful and unhelpful thoughts upon feelings and behaviours are described. The negative trap, whereby unhelpful thoughts produce unpleasant feelings that limit or restrict behaviour, is also explained.

- Psycho-education
- Introduction to the core elements of CBT, thoughts, feelings, and behaviour

Worksheets

Putting it all together is a summary of the way our thinking develops and the link between thoughts, feelings, and behaviour. *What you think, how you feel, and what you do* relates this connection to a positive event that the child really enjoyed. How this connection works with a difficult situation is explained in the *negative trap*. These two exercises can be compared to highlight the importance of the way we think. You can highlight how some ways of thinking are helpful, make us feel good, and encourage and help us to do things, whilst other ways of thinking are unhelpful, make us feel unpleasant and talk us out of doing things.

Finally, depending upon the child, how we feel could be subdivided into feelings (emotions) and body changes (physiological reactions). In most cases, this is not necessary but can be useful if the child is perceiving their emotional reactions as signs of a physical illness.

Make a film strip is a way of helping the child to identify the thoughts and feelings they experience in situations. They are asked to write down or draw a film strip of an event and then to add any thoughts or feelings they can identify.

My predictions are a way of discovering some of the assumptions the child might make whilst *thoughts, feelings, and what you do* is a puzzle that helps to distinguish between the three core elements of the CBT framework. Both can be adapted and modified to the particular child with key themes that emerge during assessment being incorporated into questions that can be introduced into the quiz.

▶ Automatic thoughts

Summary

Automatic thoughts are explained by the metaphor of a CD playing in the child's head. The cognitive triad (thoughts about me, what I do, and my future) is introduced and used to identify the different focus of their thoughts. Automatic thoughts are described as GO thoughts which are helpful, encouraging, and make the child feel pleasant. Alternatively, thoughts can also be STOP thoughts which are unhelpful, demotivating, and make the child feel unpleasant. The reasons why automatic thoughts seem so reasonable are explained, and the effects of positive and negative automatic thoughts upon feelings and behaviour explored. Finally, the need to identify 'hot' thoughts that produce strong emotional reactions is highlighted.

> ▪ Introduction to automatic thoughts and the cognitive triad
>
> ▪ Thought monitoring and identification of common negative and unhelpful thoughts

Worksheets

For older children, a 'thought and feelings' diary provides a structure for recording *hot thoughts* and linking these to feelings. If home-based monitoring is not possible, then my '*hot' thoughts* provide a way of identifying during a clinical session the common thoughts that the child may have about themselves, what they do, and their future. Similarly, STOP *thoughts* and GO *thoughts* can be used to identify some of the common thoughts the child may notice.

Structured diaries and exercises can be useful for some children, whereas others will prefer a more flexible approach. Encouraging the child to make their own diary on his or her computer or phone, to email hot thoughts to the clinician, to 'download his or her head' into a tape recorder or to simply 'catch' the occasional though when it occurs are all possibilities.

Thought bubble worksheets relating to the cognitive triad are included. The child is encouraged to draw a picture or write down some of the thoughts they have about '*me*', '*what I do*', and '*my future*'. Once again, the bubbles can be adapted to pursue important themes identified by the clinician. If young children find it difficult to verbalise their thoughts, then parents could be asked to suggest the sort of thoughts that their child may have.

For those children, who appear to have persistent difficulty in accessing their thoughts, *what are they thinking* may be helpful. The child is asked to suggest what two different characters in a picture may be thinking. *More than one thought* requires the child to generate two or three suggestions as to what thoughts one character may have. This demonstrates that there is more than one way of thinking about an event and that there is no 'right' or 'wrong' way of thinking. These worksheets provide a way of assessing whether the child is able to identify and verbalise cognitions, and introduces them to the idea of describing thoughts.

▶ Thinking traps

Summary

Cognitive distortions are introduced as thinking traps which bias the way events are perceived. Thinking traps result in positive events being overlooked or their importance minimised. Five main types of thinking traps are described. Negative filters are those where negative events are focused on whilst anything positive is overlooked (selective abstraction, disqualifying the positive). Blowing things up highlights how the importance attached to negative events is exaggerated (dichotomous thinking, magnification, and overgeneralisation). Predicting failure explains how we expect bad things to happen (arbitrary inference). With this thinking trap, we make inferences about what other people are thinking or what will happen in the future. The fourth trap is that of being down on yourself where negative labels (global labelling) are assigned to the individual or they blame themselves (personalisation) for anything that goes wrong. Finally, setting yourself to fail highlights how we often expect to be perfect and set ourselves impossible standards (unrealistic expectations). Our unrealistic standards often include words like 'should' or 'must'.

> ◼ Identification of common thinking traps
> ◼ Thought monitoring and identification of personal traps

Worksheets

Finding thinking traps is designed to help the child to capture negative thoughts and to identify the common types of cognitive distortions that they make. Once again, the process for achieving this can be adapted to the child, and if out-of-session assignments are not possible, it can be undertaken during a face-to-face meeting.

Thinking traps quiz is a short assessment covering the five common types of distortions identified in the handout. It provides a brief way to assess which type of cognitive distortions the child makes and which are his or her most common types.

▷ Balanced thinking

Summary

The child is introduced to different ways in which they can check and test their ways of thinking. These help to ensure that he/she have looked for all the evidence and that his or her thoughts are balanced and not biased. The process involves a series of concrete steps for checking the evidence that supports or disproves his or her way of thinking. This can involve gaining the perspective of another person and checking for thinking traps. This leads to the final step of cognitive restructuring where, on the basis of all the evidence, the child identifies an alternative and more balanced, thought.

> ◼ Cognitive evaluation
> ◼ Thought testing
> ◼ Cognitive restructuring
> ◼ Balanced thinking

Worksheets

What is the evidence is designed to help the child become familiar with the thought-checking process. Negative thoughts are identified and then put on trial assessed in order to determine supportive evidence, evidence that disproves them, what someone else would say if they heard them thinking this way and whether they are caught in a thinking trap.

The 4Cs offers a four-step guide to the process of thought challenging to the final stage of cognitive restructuring. The child catches a common negative thought and then checks whether they are caught in a thinking trap. They are then asked to challenge their way of thinking and to look for anything positive that they have overlooked or dismissed. On the basis of all the evidence, the young person is invited to change their thoughts to a more balanced and helpful way of thinking.

Children can become stuck in their ways of thinking and can see no alternative view. In these cases the child can be invited to adopt a third-party perspective. *How would you help a friend* asks the child what they would say to a friend if they heard them thinking like they did.

▶ Core beliefs

Summary

The concept of core beliefs is introduced and the downward arrow 'so what?' technique is used to identify them. A process for testing core beliefs by actively looking for evidence that disproves them is described. The notion of core beliefs being strong and resistant to challenge is introduced, and the need to discuss and talk with someone else advocated.

> ▪ Identification of core beliefs
> ▪ Challenging and testing core beliefs

Worksheets

Finding core beliefs is an exercise in which the child uses the downward arrow 'so what?' technique to discover their core beliefs (Burns 1980). After each statement, the child is asked 'so what? If this were true, what does this mean about you?' until the core belief is identified. Greenberger and Padesky (1995) highlight the fact that that core beliefs appear as absolute statements, such as 'I am/ have . . . ', 'others are . . . ' and so forth.

Once identified, *are my core beliefs always true* can be used to test the validity of the belief. This is achieved by searching for any evidence, no matter how small, which would suggest that the core belief is not always 100% true. Finally, *common beliefs* provide a way of assessing how strongly the child identifies with a set of 15 beliefs. This provides the clinician with an insight into the child's beliefs that can be used to help the child discover why the same difficulties keep re-occurring or why they end up caught in the same negative traps.

▶ Controlling your thoughts

Summary

This section takes the young person through a variety of different ideas and strategies that can be used to manage unhelpful thoughts. Strategies for helping the young person to redirect and divert attention away from negative cognitions and physiological symptoms (e.g. distraction, absorbing activities) are described. Ideas for stopping (thought stopping) or turning the volume down (imagery) of their negative thoughts are provided. More balanced and helpful thoughts are promoted through strategies that develop positive or coping self-talk. Finally, the child is encouraged to experiment and test their predictions to see whether their thoughts and assumptions are true.

- Distraction
- Absorbing activities
- Coping self-talk
- Positive self-talk
- Thought stopping
- Imagery
- Behavioural experiments

Worksheets

Test your thoughts and beliefs uses the process of guided discovery to help the child to design an experiment to test the validity of his/her common thoughts and beliefs. Comparing predictions with the outcome of the experiment helps to identify, challenge, and reduce the potency of unhelpful thoughts and thinking traps.

The thought challenger provides a way of a stopping common negative thoughts and replacing them with more balanced cognitions.

The development of more balanced cognitions is promoted through three exercises. *Looking for the positive* encourages children or their parents to actively seek the positive things that happen each day. This can be particularly useful for those children or parents who are overly focused on the child's failings or the things that are not right. *Positive self-talk* helps children to find and acknowledge what they have achieved rather than focusing on areas in which they have failed. Instead of looking for what has yet to be achieved, the child is encouraged to find and praise his or her successes. *Coping self-talk* helps the child to identify the thoughts that make him or her feel unpleasant and to replace these with coping self-talk which helps him or her to be successful and to feel more relaxed and less anxious. This can be very helpful and motivating when a child is planning to do something challenging.

Ways in which the child can learn to pay less attention to their unhelpful thoughts are provided in three ways. *Thought stopping* provides a simple way of snapping an elastic band to help the child stop listening to his/her negative thoughts and to refocus his/her attention. For younger children, the *worry safe* provides a practical way of thought stopping. The child makes his or her 'safe' out of a box in which he or she can deposit his or her worries. When worries arise, the child is encouraged to write or draw them and then to lock them away in his or her safe. The safe can be 'unlocked' with the therapist or the children's parents, and can be a useful way of discovering the nature and extent of the child's worries. Finally, *turn the CD off* is an imaginative exercise that builds upon the metaphor of thoughts being like a CD playing in the child's head. The child is helped to visualise the CD player in his or her head and then to imagine turning it off. If the child is troubled by repetitive images, this process can be adapted so that the child imagines themselves turning off or stopping a DVD player.

Practice being successful is another imaginative exercise designed to help the child to face challenges or difficult situations in a more positive way. The child imagines their challenge in as much detail as possible, but this time imagines him- or herself coping and being successful.

▷ How you feel

Summary

This section focuses on affective education and aims to increase awareness of different feelings and describes the common unpleasant emotions of stress, depression, and anger. The relationship between feelings, thoughts, and behaviour is highlighted.

Worksheets

The relationship between thoughts, feelings, and behaviour is highlighted through *thoughts and feelings* and *what you do and how you feel*. A number of different feelings can be introduced to the child through the *feelings word search*. After the child has found the different feelings in the puzzle he or she can be asked to identify which of these are his or her most common feelings. An alternative approach for younger children to is to ask them to draw *my feelings* on an outline of a person. The child is asked to identify and name his or her feelings, assign each a colour, and then to colour the person, showing how much of each feeling they have inside.

Older children may be helped to tune into their feelings through the *what happens when I feel . . .* worksheets. The child is asked to identify what their face and body look like and what they do when they feel *angry, sad, anxious, or happy*. Once they have described the feeling, they are asked to rate how often they have this feeling, which can then lead to a discussion exploring associated thoughts and activities. This simple exercise can be adapted to include other emotions. Those children who experience difficulty describing their own emotions may be helped to identify the feelings of another person. Pictures of people showing different emotions can be collected from newspapers and the child is then asked to guess how these people are feeling. Similarly, the clinician could role play different emotional states which the child is invited to guess.

Linking feelings to places and events can occur through *what feeling goes where* children are given a set of feelings and places and asked to draw a line between the places and how they feel when they are there. An alternative is to ask children to generate their own common feelings and the important places and events in their life. This forms the basis of *feelings and places* in which the child chooses the feeling that best describes each situation. The connection between feelings and situations/events can be further highlighted by identifying the situations/events that produce the most pleasant/unpleasant feelings.

Finally, the *thermometer* is included as a way of helping children to rate the strength of their feelings or thoughts. Noticing changes in the strength of feelings or thoughts is important since the aim is not to completely take unpleasant feelings or unhelpful thoughts away. The aim is to help the child feel more in control and to reduce the strength of these unpleasant feelings and unhelpful thoughts. Noticing changes in ratings over time is a helpful way of tracking improvements which may otherwise go unnoticed.

▶ Controlling your feelings

Summary

Practical ways of controlling unpleasant feelings are identified. Muscular physical relaxation and quick relaxation exercises are described. The child is introduced to controlled breathing and the possible calming role of naturally occurring events such as physical exercise or absorbing activities. Relaxing imagery is developed by imagining a special calming place. Finally, the metaphor of a volcano is used to explain anger and the need to prevent the volcano blowing its top.

Young children may be helped to reduce unpleasant feelings by using *the feeling strong room*. This is similar to the worry safe and involves the child making their own 'strong room', in which pictures or descriptions of unpleasant feelings can be deposited. Once again, this can be reviewed with the clinician or the child's carers in order to identify the extent and nature of the child's unpleasant feelings. Completing the thought bubbles of *my relaxing activities* may help to identify those activities that the child finds calming.

Younger children can be helped by *learning to relax*, where they are encouraged to tense and relax their muscles through a game of 'Simon Says'. Older children may find imagery more appealing, and a worksheet to enable them to identify and describe a picture of *my calming place* is included. When creating the image, it is important to describe the scene in as much detail as possible and to identify and build in a range of different sensations (e.g. sight, smell, touch).

The anger volcano can be used as a metaphor for children who experience aggressive outbursts. Children are helped to plot their own unique anger build-up by tuning into their thoughts, physiological reactions, and behaviour as they progress from being calm through to an aggressive outburst. This is sequentially plotted on to their volcano, helping them to identify their anger build-up so that they can intervene at an earlier stage to stop the volcano blowing its top.

Changing your behaviour

Summary

The way in which thoughts and feelings affect behaviour is explained. The need to become more active is emphasised, and increasing enjoyable activities is suggested as a first step. Rescheduling activities, breaking down challenges into smaller steps, graded exposure, and response prevention are identified as ways in which children can regain control of his or her life.

- Activity monitoring
- Activity re-scheduling
- Behavioural activation
- Hierarchy development
- Systematic desensitisation
- Response prevention

Worksheets

A series of worksheets in which the child has to fill in thought bubbles by writing or drawing pictures can be used to identify *things that make me feel good* and *things that make me feel unpleasant*. Identifying fun activities can be done in *have more fun*. The idea is based on the principle of behavioural activation where the child is encouraged to become busier and to build more enjoyable activities into their life.

Feelings and activity can be monitored through an *activity diary* where the child describes what he or she is doing and rates his or her mood for each hour throughout the day. This may identify particular patterns, with certain times or activities being more strongly associated with intense unpleasant feelings. This would lead into activity scheduling, where the child is encouraged to increase enjoyable activities or to explore different ways of timetabling his or her day to avoid those times associated with strong unpleasant emotions.

The idea of breaking down tasks and challenges into smaller steps to increase the likelihood of success is explained through *small steps*. The child is helped to develop a staged hierarchy with the easier, less anxiety-provoking steps being successfully completed before progressing to the next stage. For those children with obsessional habits, the *habit ladder* can be helpful. The child identifies all of their habits and then arranges them in order of difficulty with the easiest to stop at the bottom and the hardest at the top. Once again, the idea is to be successful so the child would start to boss back the easier habits at the bottom of their ladder before progressing to the next step.

Face your fears helps the child to overcome fearful challenges. The child uses small steps to systematically break their challenge into more achievable steps. They then face their fear using coping self-talk and relaxation skills to help them cope. This approach is also used in the response prevention programme *dump your habits*, in which the child is helped to gain control of his/her behaviour and to stop his/her habits. Stopping long-standing habits is difficult, and the child may need someone else present to encourage and help them.

The need for self-reinforcement and reward for success is highlighted throughout this section. *Reward yourself* encourages children to find different ways they can reward themselves to celebrate their success, no matter how small it may be.

▶ Learning to problem-solve

Summary

Three common reasons for problems are identified, namely acting without thinking, feelings taking over, or not being able to find alternative solutions. Ways of developing more effective problem-solving skills are explained, and a self-instructional traffic light model of stop, plan and go is suggested. Alternative and consequential thinking is highlighted, and ways in which new problem-solving skills can be prompted are explored. Finally, the need to practice new skills (both imaginative and in vivo) is highlighted.

> - Alternative thinking
> - Consequential thinking
> - Self-instructional training

Worksheets

Looking for solutions is a thought bubble approach that can be used to enable young children to think about different ways in which problems can be approached. Older children can be introduced to the idea of alternative thinking through *identify possible solutions* – 'OR'. The child is asked to generate as many different solutions to his or her problem as possible by ending each with the statement 'OR'. Once alternative solutions have been identified, consequential thinking can be developed through *what are the consequences?* The child is introduced to a problem-solving approach on which the positive and negative consequences of each solution are identified and assessed, to help them arrive at the best way of solving their problem. During this stage, the child should be encouraged to consider immediate and long-term consequences and the consequences for themselves and any others who may be involved. Finally, children can be encouraged to talk with or observe a successful model in *ask someone who is successful*.

A self-instructional approach to problem-solving is used to help children learn to *stop, plan, and go*. The image of a traffic light is developed to help the child learn to stop, decide on an action plan, and then implement it. Finally, *talk yourself through it* provides another means by which children can learn to solve their problems. The child is helped to internalise successful problem-solving by watching and listening to someone else coping successfully. Initially, the child talks him- or herself through this plan out loud, but over time the volume is reduced and the plan is internalised.

Be kind to yourself

We are not always very good at looking after ourselves. We are often very critical and unkind. We

▶ **beat** ourselves up

▶ **criticise** what we do

▶ **blame** ourselves for things that go wrong or

▶ feel **ashamed** if we are not perfect

From an early age, we are encouraged to be successful, to work hard, to be competitive, and to try our best. This helps to motivate us but can become a problem when we

▶ are **never satisfied** with what we do or achieve

▶ **blame ourselves** for everything that goes wrong

▶ focus on the things that **aren't right**

▶ never **acknowledge our strengths** or **celebrate our successes**

INNER VOICE

When this happens, we develop a **critical inner voice**. We are unkind to ourselves. We constantly criticise ourselves. We blame ourselves for things that aren't right. We end up feeling sad, angry, or worried.

Instead of tearing ourselves apart we need to **accept** that

▶ things will **go wrong**

▶ we **are not perfect**

▶ we **will make mistakes**

▶ **unkind things happen**

Think Good, Feel Good: A Cognitive Behavioural Therapy Workbook for Children and Young People, Second Edition. Paul Stallard.
© 2019 John Wiley & Sons Ltd. Published 2019 by John Wiley & Sons Ltd.
Companion website: www.wiley.com/go/thinkgoodfeelgood2e

Helpful Tips

We need to **be kinder** to ourselves. We need to feel comfortable with who we are, acknowledge our strengths, and to celebrate what we achieve.

Eight ways to be kind to yourself

This will probably feel odd to start with. You are used to listening to your critical inner voice so changing this may take time. Practicing these eight helpful habits will help you learn to be kinder to yourself.

Treat yourself like you would treat a friend

We are often quick to find our faults and to criticise ourselves. Our **critical inner voice** will tell us that we are "useless", "a failure" or "weak" or call us names like "stupid", "idiot" or "looser". As we beat ourselves up we end up feeling even more stressed, angry or down.

We are usually much harder on ourselves than we would be on someone else. What would you say to your friend if you heard them being very critical of themselves?

▶ If your friend says, 'No one likes me', you probably wouldn't say, 'I don't know anyone who does, including me'.

▶ If your friend said, 'I'm stupid, I can't do this work', you probably wouldn't say, 'Yes, you are very stupid, and you will never be able to do it'.

▶ If your friend was upset and said, 'Everything goes wrong for me', you probably wouldn't say, 'Yes, you are a loser, and you always will be'.

You wouldn't treat your friends like this. You would probably be

▶ **worried** about them

▶ try to **comfort** them

▶ say **kind** things

▶ and try to **cheer them up**

So stop being so down on yourself and treat yourself in the same way you would treat a friend.

When you notice your **critical inner voice**, write down what you are thinking and saying about yourself. It may feel odd but write down exactly what your critical inner voice is saying.

Now ask yourself **what you would say to your friend** if you heard them thinking and saying these things.

Treat yourself like you would treat your friends and writer a kinder and less critical message to yourself.

Helpful Tips

Instead of listening to your critical inner voice and beating yourself up try to **be kind to yourself**. Treat yourself like you would treat your friends.

Don't beat yourself up when you are feeling down

Evgenii Naumov/123RF

If you are feeling stressed, angry, or down, don't make it worse by blaming yourself for feeling so bad. You wouldn't blame yourself if you caught a cold. You would look after yourself and do something nice to help you feel better.

If you have had a difficult day and feel bad don't punish or blame yourself for what has happened or how you feel. **Care for yourself** and do something to help you feel better.

- enjoy a long relaxing bath

- play a game

- watch an episode of your favourite serial or box set

- go for a walk

- eat a slice of cake or a biscuit

- make a drink of hot chocolate

Helpful Tips

Stop beating yourself up. You don't deserve to feel like this. Look after yourself and **do something that will make you feel better**.

Forgive yourself

Our inner voice is very good at finding faults in the things we do. Instead of focusing on these and blaming ourselves for making mistakes try to **be more forgiving**. Remember

- **We all get things wrong**. Everyone makes mistakes so don't give yourself a hard time for getting something wrong. Expect things to go wrong, learn from your mistakes, and plan what you will do differently next time.

- **We all have off days**. Some days will be better than others. It is just the way it is. Try again tomorrow and see what happens.

- **Be patient**. It often takes time to get things right. You didn't learn to ride a bike, read a book, play music, or a sport straightaway. It takes time. Celebrate what you have achieved rather than criticising yourself for what you have not yet done.

Helpful Tips

Give yourself **permission to make mistakes**. Learn from what happens and decide what you will do differently next time.

Celebrate what you do

smartboy10/istock via Getty Images

We want to do well but often feel dis-satisfied with what we do. We aim too high so that we always end up failing. Instead of setting ourselves up to fail **celebrate what you do**.

- **Don't compare yourself to others**. We tend to look for the most successful person and compare ourselves against them. It is not surprising that we feel inadequate. You don't have to be better than everyone else so stop comparing yourself to others.

- **You can't always be 'the best'**. There will be many times when others are better at things than you. Famous celebrities may be good at acting, music, or sport, but there will be plenty of things they struggle to do. Focus on your strengths and don't expect to be the best at everything.

- **Avoid 'should' and 'musts'**. Words like these set us up to fail. When we say we 'should' or 'must' do something, we are really saying that what we have already done isn't right or good enough. Recognise and value what you have achieved.

- **Reward effort not success**. Focusing on outcomes can remind you of what you have not yet achieved. You probably tried to do your best so focus on your effort not the outcome.

Helpful Tips

Each day write down one or two things you **want to celebrate**. Over time, this list will grow and help you to notice and celebrate what you have achieved.

Accept who you are

We spend a lot of time thinking about our faults and how we could be different. We are often dissatisfied with ourselves and may want to be taller, slimmer, brighter, more attractive, or better at sports.

Instead of wishing you could be different **accept yourself** for who you are. Remember

- **Your qualities** – are you patient, determined, hard-working, kind, reliable, sensitive, honest, understanding, see things through?

- **Your friendships** – are you a good listener, supportive, loyal, caring, trustworthy, considerate, supportive, a good laugh?

- **Your appearance** – are you well proportioned, have a nice body shape, eyes, hair, skin, hands, nails, mouth, teeth, a nice voice?

- **Your skills** – are you good at sport, music, school work, art, drama, gaming, cooking, singing, being creative, growing things, putting on make-up, caring for animals?

Instead of focusing on the things you would like to change, **accept yourself for who you are**. Remind yourself that you are special and that there is nobody else like you.

Speak kindly to yourself

Our critical inner voice is very harsh and unkind. We say things in our heads that we would find embarrassing to speak out aloud. Try to **develop a kinder inner voice**.

Try to find one or two short 'kind' statements that work for you.

- 'I am having a hard time. Everybody finds things difficult. I need to look after myself'.

- 'I am feeling really down. Lots of people feel like me. I need to accept myself for who I am'.

- 'I am really angry. We all feel angry at times. I am trying my best to cope with this'.

Helpful Tips

Try speaking kindly to yourself at the start and end of each day. Stand in front of a mirror and say it out aloud in a kind voice.

See the good in others

When you feel anxious, angry, or down, it often feels that

▶ everyone is **picking on you** or having a go

▶ as if the world is **out to get you**

▶ these things **only happen to you**

▶ everyone is **mean or unkind**

Because you are expecting people to be unkind, you are probably looking for evidence of this. The more you look, the more you will find.

see in **GOOD** others

Try to change this by looking for the times that someone has been caring or kind. Assume the best in people and **find the kind things that happen**. Look for those times when someone

▶ makes time to talk and listen to someone

▶ says something nice like 'I like your trainers' or 'you hair looks good'

▶ is caring and gives someone a hug or makes them a drink

▶ helps by doing a chore like laying the table or doing the washing up

▶ shares something like their music or chocolate

▶ sends a kind email or text

▶ says 'thank you'

▶ makes someone laugh or smile.

Helpful Tips

Look for the good in people and find one example each day **where someone has been kind**. You might find that people are kinder than you thought.

Be kind to others

You know how good it feels when people are kind to you, so why don't you make an extra effort to **be kind to someone else**. Each day remember to give someone a compliment, smile, offer to help, or take time to listen to what they have to say.

Helpful Tips

At the end of each day, write down any of your acts of kindness and plan what you could do tomorrow **to be kind to someone**.

Remember!

Our inner voice can be very **critical** and **unkind**. Stop beating yourself up and learn to

▶ **Care** for yourself

▶ **Be Kind** to others

▶ **Accept** yourself for who you are and what you do

Remember that things will go wrong, we are not perfect, we will make mistakes, and unkind things will happen.

Don't get upset or blame yourself for what happens. Learn to accept it.

Treat yourself like a friend

We are often very unkind and critical of ourselves but would never say these sort of things to our friends.

When you notice your critical inner voice, write down exactly what you are thinking and calling yourself.

Ask yourself what you would say to your friend if you heard them thinking and saying these things.

Now treat yourself the same way and write a kinder message to yourself.

What is my critical inner voice saying?

What would I say to my friends if I heard them saying this?

What should I say to myself now?

Try to develop a kinder, less-critical inner voice.

Accept who I am

We spend a lot of time thinking about our faults and wishing that we could be different.

Try to **accept yourself** for who you are and write in the box your

▷ qualities

▷ friendships

▷ skills

▷ strengths

What is **special about me**? My qualities, friendships, skills, and strengths.

Focusing on your strengths will remind yourself that you are special.

Care for yourself

When you feel down don't beat yourself up or blame yourself for feeling so bad. Take care of yourself.

Make a list of all the treats that make you feel better.

Treats that make me feel better

When you are feeling down or had a bad day look after yourself. Have a treat and make yourself feel better.

A kinder inner voice

Our critical inner voice is very harsh and unkind so practice talking to yourself in a kinder way.

Find some short statements that recognise that you are feeling down and that you need to care for yourself.

'I am having a hard time. Everybody finds things difficult. I need to look after myself'.

Stand in front of a mirror and repeat your kinder voice out loud at the start and end of each day.

My kinder voice

My kinder voice

My kinder voice

Repeat your statements with kindness and confidence.

Finding kindness

Spend a few minutes each day to think about what has happened and find one example where

someone has been kind to you or

you have been kind to someone else

Day	What happened

Looking for kindness will help you to feel better about yourself and the people around you.

Here and now

Our minds are always busy. We spend a lot of time thinking about what has happened and worrying about what will happen.

Thinking about the past and future **can be helpful**. It helps us

▷ **learn** from what has happened to avoid future problems

▷ **change** what we do so that we will be even better next time

▷ **prepare** ourselves to deal with future events

▷ **plan** how we can cope with challenges

Sometimes, we spend too much time going over past events or worrying about the future. When this happens, our thoughts often become **unhelpful**:

▷ Keep going over and over the **bad or unfair** things that have happened.

▷ We expect things will go **wrong**.

▷ We think that we will **not cope**.

▷ We feel **anxious, sad, or angry**.

Because we spend so much time in the past or worrying about the future, we don't notice what is happening **here and now**.

Do you really notice what you do?

Did you really notice how you washed this morning? What did

▷ the soap **smell** like?

▷ the water **feel** like on your face?

Think Good, Feel Good: A Cognitive Behavioural Therapy Workbook for Children and Young People, Second Edition. Paul Stallard.
© 2019 John Wiley & Sons, Ltd. Published 2019 by John Wiley & Sons Ltd.
Companion website: www.wiley.com/go/thinkgoodfeelgood2e

Ron Leishman/Shutterstock

- the toothpaste **taste** like?

- the water **sound** like as it emptied from the sink?

- your taps **look** like?

Did you really notice your walk to school? Did you

- **hear** any cars, birds, or people talking?

- notice how your feet **felt** as you took each step?

- **see** the street signs you walked past?

- notice any **smells** of flowers, cars, or food?

Lightspring/Shutterstock

Helpful Tips

Focusing on the here and now can help you feel better and to get rid of the clutter that tumbles around your head.

FOCUS

We can train our minds to focus on what is going on around us. Like any new skill, it takes time to learn and you need to practice.

The word **FOCUS** can help remind us of the steps we need take to train our minds:

- **F**ocus your attention

- **Ob**serve what is happening

- Be **C**urious

- **U**se all your senses

- **St**ay with it

patrimonio designs ltd/ Shutterstock

Focus your attention

Imagine that you are looking through a camera with a **big zoom lens**.

- Before you look through the camera, you will find many different things to look at.

▶ As you look through the camera, your attention becomes more focused. You no longer see everything, but you see smaller things in more detail.

▶ As you zoom in, you become more focused and start to notice smaller and smaller details.

Observe *what is happening*

Look very carefully and describe what you see. Observe the

Chudomir Tsankov/123RF

▶ Shapes

▶ Size

▶ Colours

▶ Textures

Imagine this is the very first time you have ever seen these things, so really look carefully, and imagine you are describing these to someone else.

Be *curious*

As you observe, look very carefully and try to find at least one thing you have never seen or noticed before.

ColinCramm/Shutterstock

▶ If you are observing a tree, have you noticed the pattern on the tree trunk? How many branches can you see?

▶ If you are observing a sauce bottle, what does the writing on the label say? When do you need to use it by?

Be curious and ask yourself questions about the things you are observing.

▶ How long does it take for your breakfast cereal to go soggy?

▶ How many times do you move your toothbrush up and down when you brush your teeth?

We often don't really look or think about many of our everyday objects, so observe carefully and be.

Use your sense

Panptys/Shutterstock

Check out each of your senses and become aware of any

▶ Smells

▶ Sounds

- Feelings
- Sights
- Tastes

Stay *with it*

Welf Boris Weidner/123RF

You will find that your attention will wander and you will start to think about other things. Don't worry.

Training your attention to focus on the here and now is like training a puppy. Puppies like to run around, explore everything they see, and will not sit quietly by your side.

Our attention is the same. If we don't focus our attention on what we are doing, our mind will wander, and we will think about other things.

If a puppy wanders off, we call it back. We need to do the same with our attention. As soon as you notice your attention wandering, steer it back and stay with what is happening **here and now**.

FOCUS on your breathing

Memo Angeles/Shutterstock

Your breathing is a good way to practice focusing on the here and now. Choose a quiet time when you will not be disturbed for one to two minutes. Sit comfortably with your hands on your chest. You may want to shut your eyes, but that is up to you.

- **Focus** your attention on your breathing. Zoom your attention on to your nose, mouth, chest, and lungs.
- **Observe** your breathing. Breathe slowly in through your nose and out through your mouth. Notice how your chest rises and falls as you breathe in and out.
- Be **Curious**. Have you noticed anything new about the way you breathe? How many breaths do you take in 30 seconds? Does it take longer to breathe in than to breathe out? Is the air you breathe out warmer than the air you breathe in?
- **Use** your senses:
  - **Look** at the way your chest rises and falls with each breath.
  - **Listen** to the sound of your breath as you breathe in and out.
  - **Feel** the cold air in your nose as you breathe in and the warm air in your mouth as you breathe out.

> **Stay** with it. Count 1 as you breathe in and 2 as you breathe out and count up to 10.

Don't worry if you notice your mind wandering. As soon as you become aware that your mind is not focused on your breathing steer your attention back and count your breaths.

Helpful Tips

You are always breathing, so this is a very quick way to focus on the here and now. It only takes two minutes so try and practice every day.

zaricm/istock via Getty Images

FOCUS on your eating

We are often rushing around and don't really notice many of the everyday things we do. Try this exercise to help you focus on your eating.

Choose something you enjoy eating like a piece of cake, chocolate, or fruit.

> **Focus** your attention on what you are going to eat. Zoom your attention in on your food.

> **Observe** your food. Hold it in your hand and look very closely at it.

> Be **Curious**. Find something new, something you have never noticed before. How many times do you chew each mouthful? Do you chew in one part of your mouth or use it all? Can you feel your food moving down your throat to your tummy?

> **Use** your senses to explore your food:

>> What does it **look** like? What shape and colour is it? Is it shiny or dull?

>> What does it **smell** like? Does it smell? Is it sweet or is it sour?

>> What does it **feel** like? Is it hard or soft? Is it crumbly? Is it changing as you hold it?

>> Now put the food in your mouth. What does it **taste** like? Is it sweet, sour, or sharp? Is there more than one flavour?

>> What sounds you **hear** as you eat. Is there a crunch as you take each bite? Is it loud or quiet? Do the sounds change as you chew?

> **Stay** with it. Observe every chew and mouthful as if it is the very first time you have ever eaten this food. If your mind wanders off, gently steer your attention back to your food.

At the start of each meal, FOCUS on the first few mouthfuls and pretend that you have never eaten this food before.

FOCUS on an activity

You don't have to sit still to focus on the here and now. Try focusing on an everyday activity like walking. Often, when we walk our mind is somewhere else and we never really notice what is happening.

▷ **Focus** your attention on your walking and zoom in on your feet.

▷ **Observe** each step you take and notice:

  ▷ How you lift one foot whilst the other stays on the ground.

  ▷ The pressure on the bottom of your foot.

  ▷ How your foot presses against your shoe or sock.

  ▷ How your foot becomes lighter as you lift it.

  ▷ The feeling of the ground beneath your shoe.

▷ Be **Curious**. How many muscle movements are involved in each step? How long is each step? What foot do you start walking with?

▷ **Use** your senses to focus on your walking:

  ▷ Zoom in on what you **see**. Notice the colours, shapes, size, and patterns of the things you walk past.

  ▷ Zoom in on what you **hear**. Focus on the sounds of the wind, the rain, the birds, and the cars.

  ▷ Zoom in on what you **feel**. Focus on the hot or cold feeling on your face, your bag feeling heavy on your shoulder, and the rough stones beneath your feet.

  ▷ Zoom in on what you **smell**. The damp smell from the rain, the sweet smell of the flowers, and the smell of food cooking.

▷ **Stay** with it. If you notice your mind wander guide it back to your walk. Stay with it for at least 10 steps.

FOCUS on one activity each day. Choose any everyday activity like how you get out of bed, make a drink, get dressed, or check your phone and discover what you really do.

Zern Liew/Shutterstock

FOCUS on an object

We often don't really notice many of the everyday things we use or see. Try drawing a picture of your TV controller, phone, or laptop. Now have a close look and see how much detail you have missed.

Choose one thing each day and focus on it. It can be anything that is around you like

▷ Your pen

▷ Your phone

▷ A cup or plate

▷ A toothbrush

▷ Your house key

▷ A sauce bottle

▷ The bus or train you are travelling on

▷ The tree outside your window

Use the FOCUS steps to explore your object for one minute.

Helpful Tips

This is something you can do any time any place. Really FOCUS on the object and explore it as if it is the very first time you have ever seen it.

Step back from your thoughts

We often keep thinking about what has happened or worrying about what will happen and this can make our thoughts seem **very powerful**. This is because of the following:

▷ we listen to our thoughts so often that we **accept** them as real.

▷ they seem reasonable and so we **rarely question** or challenge them.

▷ we **look for evidence**, no matter how small, to prove they are right.

▷ Because we have these thoughts we **believe that they must be true**.

What **we forget** is the following:

▶ **You create** the thoughts that tumble around in your head. This is the way you think about the things that have or will happen.

▶ **They come and go** and as one thought passes another takes its place. Our minds are always busy and thoughts will automatically pop into your head.

▶ They often **don't tell the whole story**. Many of the thoughts that keep going round in our heads focus on negative things.

▶ What you think is **often not reality**. Just because you think it does not mean that it will happen.

Helpful Tips

Step back from your thoughts. Notice what you are thinking, but see them for what they are. They are thoughts you have created which will come and go.

Thought spotting

Your thoughts are like trains or cars that pass through busy stations or roads. As you stand and watch on the railway platform or road you will see trains and cars come and go:

▶ Some pass through very quickly, others are slow.

▶ Some you notice, whilst others you pay less attention to.

▶ Some are long or brightly coloured, others short or don't stand out.

▶ Some are the same, and others are different.

Try **thought spotting**. FOCUS on what you are thinking and imagine that the thoughts that are tumbling around your head are like trains and cars. Notice how some thoughts

▷ will pass through your head quickly, but others will take longer

▷ may make you feel unpleasant others won't

▷ may stick in your head whilst others don't

▷ are very similar

- **Step back** and spot your thoughts.
- Notice them **come and go**.
- **Don't react** to them or argue with them.
- Notice them, and **let them pass**.

This may seem strange to start with, so don't worry. As you practice you will find it easier to observe your thoughts. The key is to notice them, but not to argue or react to them.

Step back from your feelings

A lot of our unpleasant feelings come from thinking about the past or worrying about the future. Sometimes, our emotions feel **really strong and take over**. They boss us around and control what we do.

- When you feel anxious, you may **avoid** doing things which you really want to do.
- When you feel sad, you may **stop** going places or stay at home on your own.
- When you feel angry, you may **argue** and fall out with your friends.

We may start to have a downer on ourselves for feeling like this. We judge ourselves. Because you feel

- anxious you might criticise yourself for being **weak**.
- sad you might start to think of yourself as a **loser**.
- angry you might worry that you are a **horrible** person.

In the same way that we can step back from our thoughts, we can also learn to step back from our feelings.

www.davethompsonillustration.com

Let them float away

Emotions come and go throughout the day. Sometimes, we don't notice them, and at other times, they are strong and seem to last a long time.

They are like clouds floating in the sky or waves breaking on the beach. As one passes, another takes its place. Imagine that your emotions are like clouds or waves. Notice how some feelings

▶ **pass quickly**, and others stay longer

▶ make you **feel unpleasant**, others won't

▶ may **keep coming back**, and others don't

Step back and observe your feelings.

▶ Notice them **come and go**. Write their names on clouds in the sky, or each wave and watch them float away.

▶ **Don't react**. Don't try and stop them. Let them come.

▶ **Don't judge** yourself.

▶ Notice them and **let them pass**.

We all have feelings. The problem is that sometimes these take over, and we judge ourselves for the way we feel. Practice letting them go.

We spend a lot of time thinking about what has happened, what will happen, and don't notice what is happening **here and now**.

Focusing on the here and now can help you feel better and to get rid of the clutter in your head.

▶ **FOCUS** on what you do.

▶ **Step back** from your thoughts and emotions and let them pass.

▶ You don't need to stop or argue with them. **They are not 'facts'**, and they **do not control you**.

FOCUS on your breathing

You can use this short exercise as many times as you like each day.

Choose a quiet time where you will not be disturbed for one to two minutes. Sit comfortably with your hands resting gently on your chest.

▶ **Focus** your attention on your breathing. Zoom your attention to your nose, mouth, chest, and lungs.

▶ **Observe** your breathing. Notice how your chest rises and falls as you breathe in and out.

▶ Be **Curious**. Find one new thing about your breathing that you didn't know.

▶ **Use your Senses**:

   ▶ Look at your chest rise and fall with each breath.

   ▶ Listen to the sound of your breath.

   ▶ Feel the cold air in your nose as you breathe in and the warm air in your mouth as you breathe out.

▶ **Stay with it**. Count 1 as you breathe in and 2 as you breathe out.

▶ Count up to 10 and really **FOCUS** on your breathing.

Don't worry if you mind wanders. As soon as you notice it, bring your attention back to your breathing.

FOCUS on your eating

At the start of each meal, **FOCUS** on the first few mouthfuls of your food.

▷ **Focus** your attention on your food. Zoom your attention to the food and your mouth.

▷ **Observe** your food. Examine your food very carefully and observe what it looks like.

▷ **Be Curious**. Discover one new thing about the food or the way you eat.

▷ **Use your Senses**:

  ▷ What does your food look like? The shape, colour, and size.

  ▷ What does your food smell like? Sweet, sour.

  ▷ What does your food feel like? Hard or soft, crumbly, or chewy.

  ▷ What does your food taste like? Does it have a taste? Is it strong, or weak?

  ▷ What sounds do you hear as you chew your food?

▷ **Stay with it**. Chew each mouthful slowly, and really FOCUS on your food.

FOCUS on the first three mouthfuls of each meal. If your attention wanders off, gently steer it back to your food.

FOCUS on an object

Make a list of familiar everyday objects, and chose one to **FOCUS** on each day for one minute.

▶ **F**ocus your attention.

▶ **O**bserve what is happening.

▶ Be **C**urious.

▶ **U**se all your senses.

▶ **S**tay with it.

Day	My object	What have I noticed?

FOCUS and find something new that you haven't noticed before.

Make a clutter jar

You can make a clutter jar as a way of showing all the thoughts racing through your mind.

Find an empty jar with a screw top and fill it to the top with bottled water.

Stir some glitter into the water, put on the top, and give it a shake.

Decide whether you are happy with the effect or whether you want to add anymore glitter.

You can use your clutter jar to help you **STEP BACK** from your thoughts:

▷ Imagine that the jar is your head and the glitter your thoughts.

▷ Give the jar a shake and watch the glitter swirl around.

▷ The jar becomes busy as all your thoughts fly around.

▷ Keep swirling the jar and notice what thoughts are swirling around your head.

▷ Now put the jar down and watch carefully as the glitter sinks to the bottom of the jar and the water clears.

▷ The glitter is still there in the bottom of the jar, but you can now see through the jar.

▷ Your thoughts are still there, but they are no longer cluttering your head.

Step back and observe your thoughts. They will settle, and your mind will clear.

Thought spotting

Make a time each day to go thought spotting.

▶ Find a place to sit quietly, and FOCUS on your breathing.

▶ Take three breaths, and FOCUS on each breath as you breathe in and out.

▶ Now ZOOM in on your thoughts.

▶ Notice the thoughts tumbling around your head and **STEP BACK** from them.

▶ Don't argue with them or become upset by them.

▶ Your thoughts are like trains passing through a station.

▶ They are like cars driving past you on a road.

▶ Notice how some thoughts pass through quickly but others take longer.

▶ Notice how some thoughts are big and powerful and take over.

▶ Notice them, but don't argue or react with them. STEP BACK from your thoughts.

▶ They are your thoughts. You created them. They are not facts, and your thoughts do not control you.

Don't let your thoughts take over and boss you around. STEP BACK from them. Don't argue or react to them. Let them pass.

Let feelings float away

When you notice your unpleasant feelings becoming very powerful try to **STEP BACK** from them

▶ Find a place to sit quietly, and FOCUS on your breathing.

▶ Take three breaths and FOCUS on each breath as you breathe in and out.

▶ Now ZOOM in on your feelings.

▶ Check out how you are feeling, and **STEP BACK** from them.

▶ Watch or imagine clouds floating in the sky, or waves crashing on the beach.

▶ Imagine yourself writing the name of each feeling on a cloud or wave.

▶ Watch as the cloud drifts past, and the wave crashes on the beach.

▶ Like you feelings, clouds, and waves will keep coming.

▶ Don't try and stop them. Let the feelings come.

▶ Notice them, but **STEP BACK**, and don't judge yourself for feeling as you do.

Don't judge yourself by how you feel. STEP BACK from your feelings and watch them come and go.

CHAPTER SIX

Thoughts, feelings, and what you do

Hassles and problems are part of everyday life. Parents, friends, school, and home - in fact almost everything - create problems at some time or another.

Luckily, we are good at coping with many of these problems, and they are quickly and successfully sorted out.

Other problems seem more difficult. This may be because they

- happen fairly often
- have been around for some time
- feel totally overwhelming
- seem to affect everything you do

Sometimes these problems take over and life becomes one big unhappy worry.

Thoughts, feelings, and what you do

Think Good, Feel Good will help you to discover ways of dealing with your problems. It is based on a way of helping called **Cognitive Behavioural**

Think Good, Feel Good: A Cognitive Behavioural Therapy Workbook for Children and Young People, Second Edition. Paul Stallard.

Companion website: www.wiley.com/go/thinkgoodfeelgood2e

Therapy (CBT). This is an effective way of helping people to deal with their problems, and explores the important link between:

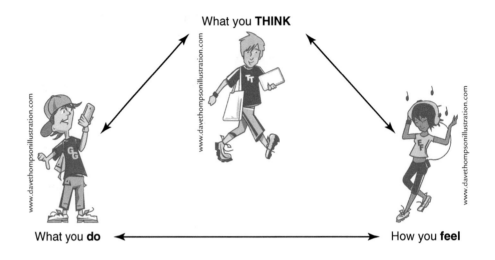

Understanding more about this link can help you to feel better and will help you to do the things you really want to do.

How does it work?

We shall find out more about this link, although the following examples may help you understand how it works:

▶ **Thinking** that you are not very good at talking with people may make you **feel** very worried or anxious when you are out with friends. You may go quiet and **not talk** very much.

▶ **Thinking** that no one likes you may make you **feel** sad. You may not want to go out and **stay at home** on your own.

▶ **Thinking** that you never get things right may make you **feel** angry. You may **give up trying** because 'it will be wrong'.

Often, as in these examples, our thoughts magically seem to come true. But **is this really the case?** Is our future so clearly set out that we are able to correctly predict what is going to happen?

Think Good, Feel Good will help you explore this question and help you realise that sometimes you may not see the whole picture. You may focus upon only one side of the story – usually that bit which has gone wrong or isn't quite right.

Often, you may not even realise what you are doing. It has become part of everyday life and it can be very difficult to see any way out or to think about how things could be different.

Because of this you will probably need the help of the **Think Good, Feel Good Team**

The Thought Tracker will help you look at the **way you think**.

The Feeling Finder will help you discover the **way you feel**.

The Go Getter will help you understand more about how you behave and **what you do**.

Helpful Tips

Think Good, Feel Good will help you learn that the way you think and approach problems will affect what happens. Perhaps you can gain greater control over what happens in your life than you really think!

What you think

Our minds are always busy. As soon as one thought passes through, another arrives to take its place. We are constantly thinking about all sorts of things. Many of our thoughts are describing what is going on around us. Others will be about ourselves.

These might be about the **way we see ourselves**:

▶ *I am fat.*

▶ *I have lots of friends.*

▶ *I've got a bad temper.*

They might be **about how we judge what we do**:

▶ *I'm hopeless at organising myself.*

▶ *I'm good at sports.*

▶ *I'm pretty good at making friends.*

They might describe **our view of the future**:

▶ *No one will ever want to go out with me.*

▶ *I'll never get to university.*

▶ *I'll be a millionaire by the time I'm 30 years.*

Core beliefs

The way we think about ourselves, judge what we do, and view our future develops over time into strong patterns of thinking. These patterns of thinking are fairly fixed and become our **core beliefs**. These are often very short statements such as

▶ *I am kind.*

▶ *I work hard.*

▶ *I am successful.*

Beliefs and predictions

Core beliefs are helpful. They help us **predict** and **make sense** of what happens in our lives. They lead us to assume that certain things will happen. This is the **'IF/THEN'** link.

▶ **IF** *'I am kind'* (core belief), **THEN** other people will like me (prediction)

> IF *'I work hard'* (core belief), **THEN** I will get a good job (prediction)

> IF *'I am successful'* (core belief), **THEN** I will be happy (prediction)

Unhelpful beliefs and predictions

Many of our core beliefs are useful, but others are less helpful. They prevent us from making real choices and decisions and can lead us to make false predictions about our life. Examples of unhelpful core beliefs might be

canbedone/Shutterstock

> *Everything I do must be perfect*

> *I always get things wrong*

> *No one will ever love me*

Core beliefs such as these often set you up to **fail**, make you **feel bad**, and **limit what you do**. They lead you to predict that negative things will happen.

> The **belief** that *'everything I do must be perfect'* may lead you to **predict** that your work is never good enough. This may result in you feeling stressed and unhappy as each piece of work is repeated again and again.

> The **belief** that *'I always get things wrong'* may lead you to **predict** that there is no point in working hard. You may feel sad and become unmotivated or lose interest in your work.

> The **belief** that *'No one will ever love me'* may lead you to **predict** that people are out to make fun of you. You may feel angry and become very rude and aggressive.

Core beliefs are strong and fixed

Core beliefs are usually very strong and become fairly fixed. They are often resistant to any alternative challenge. Any **evidence that would question them** is often **ignored or dismissed** as unimportant.

> The girl who believes that *'No one will ever love me'* may reject any signs of affection from her parents as *'they don't really care – they are just trying to get round me'*.

▶ Anything, no matter how small, that supports these beliefs is seized upon as proof. The parent who has had a busy day and has not had time to wash that special item of clothing maybe seen as evidence that *'I knew you didn't care about me'*.

Important events

These core beliefs and predictions are always there, but they come to the front of our thinking at certain times. They are often triggered by **important events** or experiences:

▶ Being asked to complete your GCSE course work may trigger the core belief that *'everything I do must be perfect'* and the prediction that *'I never get it quite right'*.

▶ Failing a test may trigger the core belief that *'I always get things wrong'* and the prediction that *'There is no point in trying again'*.

▶ Falling out with a friend could trigger the core belief that *'No one likes me'*, and the prediction that *'People are out to hurt me'*.

Automatic thoughts

Thoughts

Once triggered, core beliefs and prediction produce **automatic thoughts**.

These thoughts flood into our heads and provide us with a running commentary about what is going on.

Many of these thoughts are about ourselves, and a number of them will be negative and critical.

▶ Being asked to complete your course work may trigger automatic thoughts like *'I don't know what to do'*; *'This isn't good enough'*; or *'I'm sure that they want more than this'*.

▶ Failing your test may result in automatic thoughts like *'I really screwed this up'*; *'I'll never be able to do this'*; or *'I might as well give up'*.

▶ Falling out with your friend may result in automatic thoughts like *'I knew this wouldn't last, it never does'*; *'He/she was just making fun of me'*; or *'I'll never get another friend'*.

How you feel

As we have begun to see, the way in which we think affects how we feel. Our thoughts will result in many different **feelings**.

Helpful thoughts often produce **pleasant feelings**.

> ▶ The thought *'I'm really looking forward to that party'* may make you feel happy.

> ▶ The thought *'Although we lost I played really well'* may make you feel pleased.

> ▶ The thought *'I like good in these clothes'* may make you feel relaxed.

At other times we may have more **unhelpful** thoughts, and these often produce **unpleasant feelings**.

> ▶ The thought *'No one will turn up to my party'* may make you feel anxious.

> ▶ The thought *'We lost again – we will never win'* may make you feel angry or sad.

> ▶ The thought *'I don't like these clothes'* may make you feel worried and unhappy.

Many of these feelings will not be strong and will not last for very long. You may not even notice them.

At other times, these unpleasant feelings take over. They become very strong and seem to last.

The unpleasant feelings people notice most often are those of stress, unhappiness, and anger.

What you do

If these feelings last or become very strong, they start to have an effect on what you do. We like to feel good, so we usually try to do more of those things that make us feel good and less of those things that make us feel unpleasant.

- If you **feel anxious** when talking with other people, you may **avoid going out** or turn down invitations to meet up and do things with your friends. When you stay on your own, you may feel more relaxed.

- If you feel **sad or unhappy** at school, you may **stop going**. You may feel happier when you stay at home.

- If you **feel angry** when people criticise your work, you **may give up** trying so hard.

There are lots of ways in which your thoughts and feelings can affect what you do. You may notice that you

- **give up** and stop doing things

- **avoid** situations that might be difficult

- become **reluctant to try** new things

It would seem that these changes **prove that our thoughts were right** all along.

- Difficulty in concentrating would prove the thought that *'I will never pass these exams'*.

- Staying at home would prove the thought that *'Nobody likes me – I haven't any friends'*.

- Finding it difficult to sleep or putting on weight would prove the thoughts that *'I look terrible'*.

STOP!

Can we look at this again? **You may be caught in a trap**. You may **only** be looking for evidence to support your negative thoughts.

- You may have found it difficult to concentrate today – you didn't sleep very well last night. Usually, you sleep better, and when you have had a good night's sleep, you are able to concentrate.

- You may have stayed at home last night, but you have arranged to go out with your friends tomorrow.

- You may have gained 2 kg but does that really make such a big difference to how you look? Your favourite clothes still fit well.

Thoughts may magically come true because you are only looking for evidence that supports them. Is it possible that you are only seeing **one side of the story?**

We need to break out of this unhelpful cycle.

We need to learn to identify, question, and test some of our unhelpful thoughts.

Learning to develop a more balanced way of thinking will make you feel better and will enable you to make real choices about the important things in your life.

Putting it all together

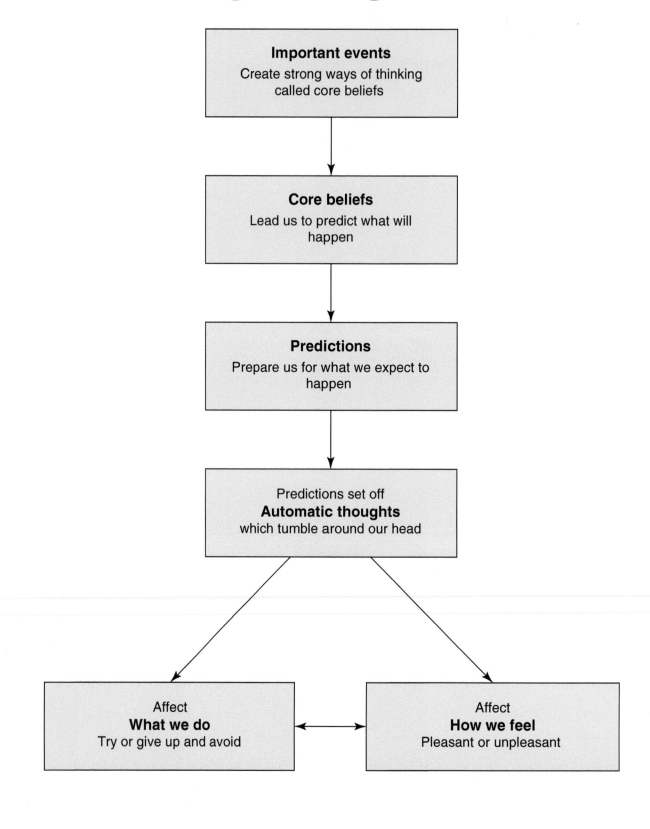

Important events
Create strong ways of thinking
called core beliefs

Core beliefs
Lead us to predict what will
happen

Predictions
Prepare us for what we expect to
happen

Predictions set off
Automatic thoughts
which tumble around our head

Affect
What we do
Try or give up and avoid

Affect
How we feel
Pleasant or unpleasant

What you think, how you feel, and what you do

Think about something you have done recently which you **really enjoyed**. Write or draw in the circles below:

▷ What you **DID**

▷ How you **FELT**

▷ What you were **THINKING**

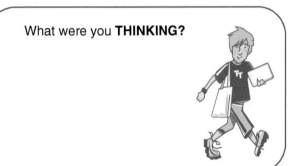

What were you **THINKING?**

What were you **DOING?**
Place people, activity

How did you **FEEL?**

The negative trap

Think about one of your **most difficult situations** and write/or draw in the circles below:

▶ What did you **Happens**

▶ How you **FEEL**

▶ What you **THINK** about when you are in that situation.

What I **THINK**

What I **DO**

How I **FEEL**

Make a film strip

Imagine that you are filming a situation that you find difficult. Start by drawing in the film sections below what happened just before, during, and immediately afterwards.

Now add the feelings and the thoughts that were tumbling through your mind.

My feelings   **What happened**   **My thoughts**

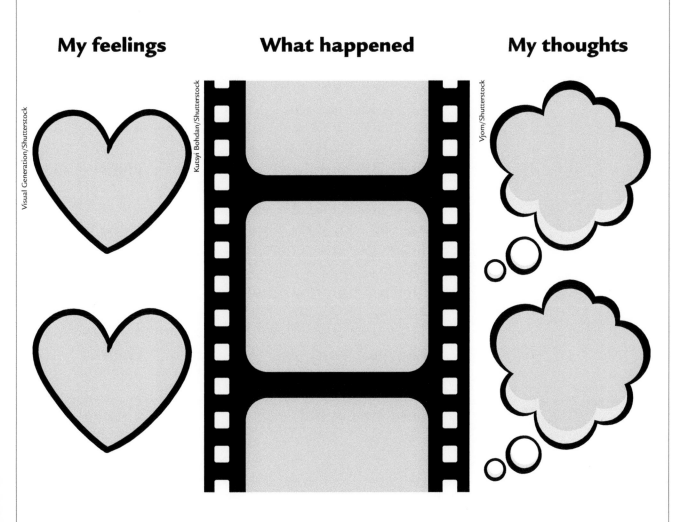

My predictions

Try the If/Then quiz. What do you think will happen?

If   I am good   **Then**

If   I get into trouble   **Then**

If   I get things wrong   **Then**

If   I work hard   **Then**

If   I have no friends   **Then**

If   People like me   **Then**

If   I make people happy   **Then**

If   I let my parents down   **Then**

If   I am not kind   **Then**

If   I am successful   **Then**

Thoughts, feelings, or what you do?

Are these **THOUGHTS**,

FEELINGS,

or, what you **DO**?

- I am going to get this wrong
- Angry
- Sad
- Going to school
- Playing with my friends
- This is really good
- I'm good at making people laugh
- Cross
- Being on my own
- People don't like me
- Having a bath
- Happy
- Eating tea
- No one will ever want to be my friend
- Stressed
- Frightened
- I will never pass my exams
- Shopping

www.davethompsonillustration.com

Automatic thoughts

The thoughts that pop into your head throughout the day are called **automatic thoughts**. They provide you with a running commentary about what happens and what you do. We have these thoughts all the time, and they are important because they affect what we do and how we feel.

Me, what I do, and my future

The automatic thoughts we are most interested in are those that are about **YOU**. They might be about any of the following.

ElenaShow/Shutterstock

▷ **How you see yourself**
I'm clever.
I'm not very good at making friends.
I'm good-looking.

Firebach/istock via Getty Images

▷ **The way you judge yourself**
Everything I do goes wrong.
I'm hopeless at sport.
I did really well in my maths test.

Mega Pixel/Shutterstock

▷ **The way you see the future**
One day I'll settle down.
I'm never going to be happy.
There are plenty of things I can do when I leave school.

These are the building blocks that shape how you see yourself. These thoughts shape what you think about yourself, how you judge what you do, and what you expect will happen in the future.

Think Good, Feel Good: A Cognitive Behavioural Therapy Workbook for Children and Young People, Second Edition. Paul Stallard.
© 2019 John Wiley & Sons Ltd. Published 2019 by John Wiley & Sons Ltd.
Companion website: www.wiley.com/go/thinkgoodfeelgood2e

These thoughts can be **positive** like

▶ *I played well in that game.*

▶ *I had a really nice time with my friends tonight.*

▶ *Mike seems to like me.*

These are **GO** thoughts which are **helpful** and **encourage** you to

▶ continue training and playing sport

▶ make another arrangement to go out with your friends

▶ invite Mike round and spend more time with him

Helpful Tips

GO thoughts are helpful and encourage you to try and face your challenges.

Automatic thoughts can also be **negative** like

▶ *That's the worst I've ever played.*

▶ *None of my friends are talking to me tonight.*

▶ *I'm not sure, but I don't think Mike likes me.*

These are **STOP** thoughts which are **unhelpful** and make you **stop or avoid** doing things. You might start to

▶ miss training sessions

▶ become less interested in going out and seeing friends

▶ avoid going to places if you know that Mike might be there

Helpful Tips

STOP thoughts are unhelpful. They make you feel unpleasant, and you will avoid or stop doing things.

We have a mixture of negative and positive automatic thoughts. Most people are able to see **both sides** and end up making **balanced decisions and judgements**.

Others find it harder to think about things positively. They seem to look through **negative glasses** and will only see and hear the things that are not right.

lineartestpilot/
Shutterstock

▶ Their thoughts tend to be very negative.

▶ They find it hard to think, hear, or see anything good about themselves.

▶ They do not recognise any positive skills.

▶ They have a gloomy view about their future and do not believe that they could be successful.

For some people, this way of thinking takes over. Their automatic thoughts become mainly negative.

Why do I listen to my automatic thoughts?

To understand this, we need to learn a little more about negative automatic thoughts. They have a number of things in common.

▶ **Automatic** – they just happen. They pop up without you having to think of them.

▶ **Distorted** – when you stop and check you will find that they don't really fit all the facts.

▶ **Continuous** – you do not choose to have them, and they can't be turned off.

▶ **Seem true** – they seem to make sense, so you accept them as true without stopping to challenge and question them.

Helpful Tips	Automatic thoughts are always tumbling through our minds. We often accept them as true even though they don't fit all the facts.

Because our automatic thoughts seem reasonable, we **listen** to them.

We become **very familiar** with them because we hear them so often.

The more we hear them, the more we **believe** and accept that they are true.

dedMazay/Alamy Stock Photo

Our negative thoughts are like a CD playing in our head:

▷ The thoughts go round and round.

▷ The CD never gets changed.

▷ The volume is never turned down.

▷ The tape is never heard by anyone else.

The negative trap

These negative automatic thoughts become unhelpful, and we can end up becoming caught in a **negative trap**.

▷ Our negative thoughts make us **feel unpleasant**.

▷ Our unpleasant feelings **prevent** us from doing things.

▷ Doing less gives us **more time to think** about all the things that are going wrong.

▷ This **confirms** our negative thoughts.

▷ And so it goes **on and on and on**.

We need to break out of the negative trap. We need to learn more about the way we think, how our thoughts make us feel, and the effect they have on what we do.

'Hot' thoughts

We have automatic thoughts all the time. However, we need to identify those that occur most often and those that are the strongest. In order to do this, we will need the help of the **Thought Tracker**.

As we have already seen, our automatic thoughts usually seem fairly reasonable. We often accept them as true without stopping to question them. In fact, we often don't even notice them. We need the **Thought Tracker** to help us to identify those thoughts that are negative and unhelpful. The **Thought Tracker** will help us to check whether we are seeing the whole story or whether we are only focusing on one small part of what is going on.

The best place to start is to look for those thoughts that stir up the strongest feelings. These are the **'HOT'** thoughts. Think about those times when you really notice a change in how you feel. Try to identify what thoughts are going through your mind when you feel like this. The following questions may help.

▷ What were you thinking **as you started** to feel this way?

▷ What were your thoughts when this feeling **became really strong?**

▷ What did you think **was going to happen?**

▷ How did you think this **would end?**

▷ What did you think **other people might say** about what happened?

Sara becomes uptight

Sara was waiting at the bus stop when she noticed herself suddenly becoming very uptight and tearful. The **Thought Tracker** helped Sara to identify the **'HOT'** automatic thoughts that were racing through her mind at the time.

▷ *What were you thinking as you started to feel this way?* Sara was thinking about the boy she had met at the disco last night. She liked him and was looking forward to meeting him again. Sara then started to worry that he wouldn't turn up.

▶ *What were your thoughts when your feelings became very strong?* Sara was now thinking of all the possible reasons why he might not turn up. She thought *'he didn't seem that keen on me when we left'*; *'he didn't ask for my telephone number'*; *'I bet he was just being polite — he didn't really want to meet me again'*.

▶ *What did you think was going to happen?* Sara was convincing herself that the boy would not turn up.

▶ *How did you think this would end?* Sara thought that she would end up in town all on her own.

▶ *What did you think other people would say?* Sara had made a big fuss about this boy, and her friends would be keen to know what happened. She started to worry about how she would explain it, and she thought that they would all laugh at her.

This negative scene was being acted out in Sara's mind. The more she had these thoughts, the worse she felt, and the more convinced she became that this would actually happen.

It is not surprising that Sara felt so uptight and sad. It all started to make sense.

davib/Shutterstock

Remember!

We have a constant stream of automatic thoughts racing through our heads.

Many of these thoughts are about ourselves, what we do, and what we expect to happen in the future.

Some of these thoughts will be negative and unhelpful and will make us feel unpleasant.

Identifying our negative and unhelpful thoughts is the first step towards learning how to feel good.

'Hot' thoughts

You need to find out more about your unhelpful negative thoughts and the effect they have on you.

Fill in the diary over the next week any time you notice a strong negative **'HOT'** thought, or if you notice a strong unpleasant feeling. When this happens, write down the following.

▷ The day and time

▷ Describe what was happening, who was there, and when and where it happened.

▷ What were your hot thoughts? What was racing through you mind at the time? Write down exactly what you thought, and don't be embarrassed.

▷ How did this make you feel?

Day and Time	What were you doing?	What were your hot thoughts?	How did you feel?

Don't worry about spelling or writing. As long as you can remember or read what you have written, it doesn't matter.

My 'hot' thoughts

Over the next week, carefully check your negative 'hot' thoughts and write down the three that you have most often about the following.

Yourself

1.

2.

3.

What you do

1.

2.

3.

Your future

1.

2.

3.

STOP thoughts

Some of our thoughts can be unhelpful. They make us feel unpleasant and STOP us from doing the things that we would really like to do.

When you notice any unhelpful thoughts, write them in the thought bubbles below.

GO thoughts

Some of our ways of thinking are helpful. They make us feel good and encourage us to do things.

When you notice any helpful thoughts write them in the thought bubbles below.

S. Hanusch/Shutterstock

Thoughts about me

Fill in the thought bubbles by writing or drawing the thoughts you have about yourself.

Thoughts about the future

Fill in the thought bubbles by writing or drawing the thoughts you have about the future.

Thoughts about what I do

Fill in the thought bubbles by writing or drawing the thoughts you have about what you do.

THINK GOOD, FEEL GOOD

What are they thinking?

Fill in the thought bubbles by writing or drawing what they might be thinking.

Fill in the thought bubbles by writing or drawing what the cat and mouse might be thinking.

More than one thought

People often have a number of thoughts. Draw or write in the thought bubbles what this person might be thinking.

Fill in the thought bubbles by writing or drawing what the cat may be thinking about the dog.

Thinking traps

www.davethompsonillustration.com

We have begun to see that some of our automatic thoughts are not very helpful. They may make us feel unpleasant or prevent us from doing things.

The problem with negative automatic thoughts is that they continue to go round and round in our heads, and we seldom stop to challenge or question them. In fact, we do the opposite – the more we hear them, the more we believe them, and the more we look for evidence or select things to prove them right.

These are **thinking traps**, and there are five types of thinking traps we need to look out for.

Negative filter

With this trap, we only focus on the negative things that happen. We only see the things that **go wrong or aren't right**. Anything positive is overlooked, disbelieved, or thought to be unimportant. There are two common types of negative filters.

lineartestpilot/
Shutterstock

Negative glasses

Negative glasses only let you see one part of what happens – the negative part.

If you have a good time, and if nice things happen, the negative glasses will still find the things that went wrong or weren't quite good enough. It is these negative things that you notice and remember most.

▶ You may have had a really good day out with your friends, but at lunchtime, your favourite cafe was full. When asked whether you had a good time, you reply, 'No. We couldn't get in the cafe'.

Think Good, Feel Good: A Cognitive Behavioural Therapy Workbook for Children and Young People, Second Edition. Paul Stallard.
© 2019 John Wiley & Sons Ltd. Published 2019 by John Wiley & Sons Ltd.
Companion website: www.wiley.com/go/thinkgoodfeelgood2e

Positive doesn't count

With this thinking error, anything positive is dismissed as unimportant or else discredited.

▸ The person who hears that a boy or girl wants to be their friend may think, *'They probably can't find anyone else to be friends with'*.

▸ Doing well in a maths test may be discounted as you think, *'But it was easy – we learned all that last year'*.

▸ Being told you did well in a sports game may be rubbished as *'I didn't play as well as Mike and Joe. They were fantastic'*.

Helpful Tips

The negative filter only allows you to notice the things that go wrong or aren't right. Try and find the positive things that you are not noticing.

Blowing things up

The second types of thinking traps are those where any negative things are blown up and **become bigger** than they really are. This happens in three main ways:

All-or-nothing thinking

Everything is seen in all-or-nothing terms. It is either boiling hot or freezing cold, and there doesn't seem to be anything in between.

▸ You may have a disagreement with your best friend and think to yourself, *'That's it – you're not my friend anymore'*.

If you fall short of perfect, then you see yourself as a total failure.

▸ Getting 72% in a maths test may cause someone to think *'I never get everything right – I'm going to give up maths'*.

Magnifying the negative

With this thinking trap, the importance of things that happen is exaggerated. Negative events are magnified and blown up out of all proportions.

> 'I forgot his name and **everyone** was looking and laughing at me'.

> 'I dropped my book and the **whole class** were watching me'.

> 'People all **always** unkind to me'.

Snowballing

With this trap, a single event or upset snowballs and quickly grows into a never-ending pattern of defeat. The first grey cloud in the sky becomes evidence of an approaching thunderstorm.

> Not being picked for the sports team could result in thoughts such as *'I'm no good at sports. I can't understand maths. I just **can't do anything'**.*

Helpful Tips — Blowing things up is where negative events become bigger than they really are. Try and keep things in perspective and recognise that it may not be as bad as you are making out.

Predicting failure

The third type of thinking traps are those that focus on the future and what we expect will happen. These traps often **predict failure** and make us expect the worse. This can happens in two main ways:

Mind reading

The mind reader thinks they know what everyone else is thinking:

> 'I know she doesn't like me.'

> 'I bet everyone is laughing at me.'

> 'My friends think I look stupid in these clothes.'

Fortune telling

The fortune teller thinks they know what will happen

> 'If we go out, I'll end up sitting on my own'.

> 'I know I'm not going to be able to do this work'.

> 'If I go to the sleep over at my friends, I won't be able to sleep'.

Predicting failure results in us expecting that we will not be successful and that things will go wrong. Try focusing on what you can do and what will be enjoyable.

Being down on yourself

With these traps, you are very **unkind to yourself**. You call yourself names and blame yourself for everything that goes wrong.

Dustbin labels

You attach a label to yourself and think of everything you do in this way.

- ‘I'm just a looser.’
- ‘I'm hopeless.’
- ‘I'm rubbish.’

Blame me

With this trap, we feel responsible for the negative things that happen, even though we have no control over them. Everything that goes wrong is down to us.

- ‘As soon as I got on the bus, it broke down.’
- If your friend doesn't see you and walks past without talking to you, you may think ‘I must have said something to upset him’.
- Your friends start to argue as you join the group may make you think ‘People always start arguing when I arrive’.

Instead of having a downer on yourself, remember your strengths and think about other reasons why things happen.

Setting yourself to fail

With this trap, we set ourselves very high standards and expectations. Often are **targets are too high**, and we are never seem able to achieve them. This can happen in two main ways:

Should and must

We sometimes think and talk to ourselves in ways that are impossible for us to achieve. They make us very aware of our failings, and the things we have not done. These often start with words such as the following:

▶ *I should.*

▶ *I must.*

▶ *I shouldn't.*

▶ *I can't.*

Expecting to be perfect

With this trap, our expectations and standards are impossibly high. Because we want to be perfect all of the time, we will be devastated when we or others fall short of our impossible standards.

▶ Because you set yourself such high standards with your schoolwork, you might be really upset or angry with a B+ or if you get anything wrong.

▶ Because you want to be a perfect swimmer, you might be devastated when you come second in a race.

▶ Because you expect your friends to be trustworthy and kind, you might be very upset when they let you down.

Helpful Tips | Revise your expectations. Recognise what you achieve rather than focusing on what you have been unable to do.

Remember!

Everyone falls into thinking traps at some time. This is normal.

The problem starts when they happen regularly and prevent you from making real choices about the things you can or want to do in your life.

Watch out for the common traps:

▶ Negative filter

▶ Blowing things up.

▶ Predicting failure.

▶ Being down on yourself

▶ Setting yourself to fail.

Finding thinking traps

When you notice a negative thought, check to see whether you have fallen into a thinking trap.

Write your thought in one of the traps below.

Negative filter

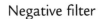

Blowing things up

Predicting failure

Being down on yourself

Setting yourself up to fail

Thinking traps quiz

Compete the quiz below to find the thinking traps you need to watch out for.

Negative filter

▶ How often do you find yourself looking for the negative things that happen?

Never   **Sometimes**   **Often**   **All the time**

▶ How often do you find yourself looking for the things that go wrong or which aren't quite good enough?

Never   **Sometimes**   **Often**   **All the time**

▶ How often do you ignore or overlook the positive or good things that happen?

Never   **Sometimes**   **Often**   **All of the time**

▶ How often do you play down the positive or good things that happen?

Never   **Sometimes**   **Often**   **All of the time**

Blowing things up

▶ How often do you find yourself using all-or-nothing thinking?

Never   **Sometimes**   **Often**   **All of the time**

▶ How often do you magnify the things that go wrong?

Never   **Sometimes**   **Often**   **All of the time**

▶ How often do single negative events snowball into something bigger?

Never   **Sometimes**   **Often**   **All of the time**

Predicting failure

▶ How often do you think you know what other people are thinking about you?

Never   **Sometimes**   **Often**   **All of the time**

▶ How often do you expect things to go wrong?

Never   **Sometimes**   **Often**   **All of the time**

Being down on yourself

▶ How often do you label or call yourself names like 'stupid' or 'loser'?

Never   **Sometimes**   **Often**   **All of the time**

▶ How often do you blame yourself for the things that happen or go wrong?

Never   **Sometimes**   **Often**   **All of the time**

Setting yourself up to fail

▶ How often do you find yourself thinking that you 'should' do this and that?

Never   **Sometimes**   **Often**   **All of the time**

▶ How often do you find yourself saying 'I must'?

Never   **Sometimes**   **Often**   **All of the time**

▶ How often do you think that things are not good enough unless they are perfect?

Never   **Sometimes**   **Often**   **All of the time**

Balanced thinking

When we become caught in thinking traps, we end up thinking in unhelpful ways over and over again.

The more we listen to our unhelpful thoughts, the more we believe them, and the harder it becomes to challenge them and to see things in a different way.

In order to break out of this cycle, we need to learn to identify and challenge our unhelpful thoughts. By doing this, we will be able to gain a more balanced view of what goes on.

Until you get used to doing it, **balanced thinking** can be hard.

The **Thought Tracker** can help you find ways to test and challenge your unhelpful thoughts.

What is the evidence?

A useful way to check and challenge your thoughts is to put them before a judge in a court of law to find the evidence to support or to question them.

Courts often ask different witnesses to provide evidence, and everything is examined in detail before a balanced verdict is made.

You can think about the people you know as your witnesses and you can look in detail at your thoughts to check whether you are caught in a thinking trap before deciding on a balanced way of thinking.

These questions will help you to check **the evidence** for your thoughts.

What is the evidence to **support** this way of thinking?

What is the evidence to **question** this way of thinking?

What would your **witnesses** (your best friend/teacher/parent) say if they heard you thinking this way?

Look at your thoughts and check whether you are caught in a **thinking trap**?

▶ Are you looking through a **negative filter** and forgetting your strengths (negative glasses or positive doesn't count)?

▶ Are you **blowing things up** and making things bigger than they really are (all or nothing thinking, magnifying the negative, or snowballing)?

▶ Are you **predicting failure** and expecting things to go wrong (mind reader or fortune teller)?

▶ Are you **being down on yourself** by being unkind or blaming yourself for things that go wrong (dustbin labels, blame me)?

▶ Are you **setting yourself to fail** with impossible standards (should and must, expecting to be perfect)?

What is **your verdict**? Is there another more balanced way of thinking about this which better fits the evidence?

Balanced thinking is **NOT** about seeing everything positively.

Your thoughts have to be realistic; otherwise, you would be pretending that everything is problem-free, and this just isn't the case.

Helpful Tips

Balanced thinking is about seeing the whole picture and looking for new information that you might otherwise overlook.

So how does it work?

Sita's schoolwork

Sita was watching TV when she noticed herself becoming very tearful and feeling very stressed. The programme on TV was one of her favourites, but she hadn't really been watching it. She was thinking about other things. The **Thought Tracker** helped Sita to find and write down the thoughts tumbling through her head:

> *I've messed everything up.*

> *I'm never going to pass my examinations.*

> *I'm just stupid.*

Now that Sita had identified the thoughts that were making her so unhappy, the next stage was to check whether she was seeing the whole story.

She decided to ask **what is the evidence** to check whether this really was balanced thinking.

> ***What is the evidence to support this way of thinking?*** Sita had been struggling to complete her maths homework that evening and no matter how she tried she just couldn't seem to do it.

> ***What is the evidence to question this way of thinking?*** Sita had never failed a maths test. None of her work this year has been lower than a C grade (a pass).

> ***What would her best friend Claire say (first witness)?*** 'You know that maths isn't your strongest subject, but you have always got through the exams. You are in the top groups for everything else'.

> ***What would her maths teacher say (second witness)?*** 'We have only recently started this work and I think it will take the class some time before they really understand it'.

> ***Examine the evidence. Is Sita caught in a thinking trap?***

1 *Negative filter*
Sita has her negative glasses on and can only think about this homework. She has overlooked that she is in the top sets for all her other subjects and that she has never failed an exam.

2 *Blowing things up*
Sita is magnifying the negative. Problems with this homework has led her to think that she has messed everything up.

3 *Predicting failure*
Sita is fortune telling and now predicting that she will not pass her examinations.

4 *Being down on herself*
Dustbin Labels Sita is using dustbin labels by calling herself 'stupid' when her friend and teachers think she is clever.

The verdict

By stopping and challenging these negative thoughts, Sita recognised that she was seeing **only half of the story**.

▶ Although she did not understand her maths homework, it was new work.

▶ Maths was her hardest subject, but so far, she had always managed to pass her exams.

▶ Finally, Sita recognised that she was doing very well in her other subjects, and there was no reason why her future would be ruined.

Adam's friends

Adam was lying in bed and felt himself becoming very tense. The **Thought Tracker** helped Adam identify the following thoughts that were racing through his head.

Mike doesn't like me anymore.

He wants to be on his own.

I'm too boring and serious.

I annoy him.

It was time for Adam to check out whether this was balanced thinking or whether he was listening only to his negative thoughts. He decided to ask himself **what is the evidence**.

▶ **What is the evidence to support this way of thinking?** Mike said he was unable to come to my house after school today. He doesn't seem very happy when we talk and often he doesn't seem to listen to what I say.

▶ **What is the evidence to question this way of thinking?** Mike slept over at my house at the weekend, and he invited me to stay with him next Saturday. I know that Mike is worried about his parents at the moment, and perhaps, he wants to stay at home with them.

▷ *What would his friend Joe say (first witness)?* 'Mike doesn't seem himself at the moment. He seems sad and is really worried about his parents'.

▷ *Examine the evidence. Is Adam caught in a thinking trap?*

1 *Predicting Failure*
Adam is mind reading by thinking that Mike doesn't like him.

2 *Being down on himself*
Adam is using dustbin labels by thinking of himself as 'boring' even though he has been friends with Mike for five years. He is also assuming that he is responsible for how Mike is behaving. There maybe another reason. Mike might be worried about his parents.

The verdict

Adam recognised that he was seeing **only half of the story**.

▷ He and Mike were still friends and had already arranged time to be together.

▷ Adam realised that maybe Mike is feeling unhappy and worried about something else rather than being fed up with him.

The 'four Cs'

Another way to check out if you have fallen into a thinking trap is to use the **'4 Cs' – catch it, check it, challenge it, change it**:

▷ **Catch** the thoughts that make you feel unpleasant or talk you out of doing things.

▷ **Check** if you are caught in a thinking trap. Are you making things out to be worse than they really are? Are you blowing things up, being down on yourself or predicting failure.

▷ **Challenge** what you are thinking by looking for evidence that questions your way of thinking. Is there something positive you have overlooked. Are you looking though a negative filter or setting yourself up to fail?

▷ **Change** to a more balanced way of thinking that makes you feel better and helps you to cope and be successful.

Check the way you are thinking by using the 4Cs. Catch the thoughts, check them, challenge them, and change them.

So how does it work?

Rocco wants new trainers

Rocco asked his mum for some new trainers, but she said no. Rocco was really angry and used the '4 Cs' to check how he was thinking.

▶ **Catch** your thoughts. What are the thoughts that are making you feel unpleasant?

Rocco was feeling angry and had lots of thoughts tumbling around his head:

I can't go out with my friends in these old trainers.

My mum hates me, she never buys me stuff.

My friends all think these trainers look stupid.

▶ **Check** your thoughts. Are you making things out to be worse than they really are?

Rocco wanted some new trainers but could see that he was **blowing things up**. He had been wearing these trainers for the past four months and his friends hadn't said anything about them.

He was **predicting failure**. He was mind reading what his friends thought about his trainers and how his mum hates him.

▶ **Challenge** your way of thinking. Is there something helpful or positive that you have overlooked?

Rocco found this hard and at the start couldn't think of anything. After a while, he noticed that he was looking though a **negative filter**. His negative glasses stopped him from seeing that his friends like him, not the things he wore. They also stopped him from seeing that Mum didn't have much money at the moment.

▶ **Change** your way of thinking.

Taking time to stop and think things through had helped Rocco to calm down and to think about this in a more balanced way.

Change it

Rocco still wanted new trainers but recognised that Mum doesn't have any money. These trainers were cool when Rocco bought them, so they can't be that bad. Perhaps his friends don't notice his trainers as much as he does.

Nikita feels left out

Nikita looked on her social networking page and found that he friends were all talking about what they had done in town last night. Nikita found herself becoming very upset. They were her friends, and they had left her out.

▶ **Catch** your thoughts. What are the thoughts that are making you feel unpleasant?

Nikita could find lots of thoughts tumbling around her head:

Everybody hates me.

Nobody wants to be with me.

I am always left out.

▶ **Check** your thoughts. Are you making things out to be worse than they really are?

Nikita was very upset and found this hard. She decided to write things down and noticed that she was *being down* on herself. Just because her friends didn't ask her to go town doesn't mean that nobody wants to be with her.

Nikita was *predicting failure* by mind reading that her friends 'hated' her. She was also *blowing things up*. She wasn't 'always' left out. She was hanging around and having a good time with her friends at school today.

▶ **Challenge** your way of thinking. Is there something helpful or positive that you have overlooked?

Nikita was looking through a *negative filter*. Her negative glasses made her think that she was 'always left out'. If they had asked her, she wouldn't have been able to go because she didn't have any money. She had forgotten that she had planned to go into town with two of her friends on Saturday.

▶ **Change** your way of thinking.

Thinking about this in a balanced way would have helped Nikita to feel better.

Change it

Nikita started to think of other reasons why her friends didn't call. Perhaps they didn't 'hate' her but didn't have time to call or forgot. This wasn't very thoughtful of them. Anyway, she had no money and had made plans to go to town with some friends on Saturday.

How would you help a friend?

Sometimes it can be hard to think about your own situation and to challenge your own thoughts. If this happens, you could try to think about how you **could help a friend** if they had your thoughts.

▶ You might have got a C grade in a test and find yourself thinking, *'I will never be able to do this work. I am an idiot'*. What would you say to your friend if they said this?

You probably **wouldn't say,** *'Yes, you are an idiot and you always get things wrong'*.

You would probably point out something that they had **overlooked or forgotten** like *'You get really good grades in art'* or *'this is the first time you have got a C'*.

▶ If you had fallen out with a friend, you might find yourself thinking, *'I am a loser, no one likes me'*. What would you say to your friend if they said this?

You probably **wouldn't say,** *'Yes, you are a loser, and I don't know anyone who likes you'*.

You would probably point out something that they had **overlooked or forgotten** like *'He seems to be arguing with everyone at the moment.*

Helpful Tips

Challenge the way you think by asking yourself what you would say to a friend if they were thinking like this.

davib/Shutterstock

Remember!

Balanced thinking is about seeing the whole picture and looking for new information that you might otherwise overlook.

You can check whether you are seeing the whole picture by

▶ asking yourself **what is the evidence?**

▶ using the '**4Cs**' – **Catch it, Check it, Challenge it, Change it**.

▶ asking what you would **say to a friend** if they were thinking like you.

What is the evidence?

You can use these questions to **check the evidence** for your thoughts and to find a more balanced way of thinking.

What are the thoughts tumbling around your head?

What is the evidence to **support** this way of thinking?

What is the evidence to **question** this way of thinking?

What would **your witnesses** (your best friend/teacher/parent) say if they heard you thinking this way?

Examine your thoughts and check whether you are caught in a **thinking trap**?

What is **your verdict**? Is there another more balanced way of thinking about this which better fits the evidence?

The '4Cs'

You can use the '**4Cs**' – Catch it, Check it, Challenge it, Change it – to check whether you are seeing the whole picture.

Catch the thoughts that make you feel unpleasant or talk you out of doing things.

Check if you are caught in a thinking trap. Are you making things out to be worse than they really are? Are you blowing things up, being down on yourself, or predicting failure?

Challenge what you are thinking. Is there something positive you have overlooked. Are you looking though a negative filter or setting yourself up to fail.

Change to a more balanced way of thinking which makes you feel better and helps you to cope and be successful.

How would you help a friend?

It can be easier to think about **what you would say** to someone else if they had thoughts like yours. We are often kinder to others and help them to notice things that they have overlooked or forgotten.

> What are the thoughts tumbling around your head?

> What would you say to your friend if they had these thoughts?

Core beliefs

Core beliefs are the fixed statements/ideas that we have about ourselves. They help us to predict what will happen and help us to make sense of our world. These core beliefs are formed in childhood, and our early experiences develop them into strong and rigid ways of thinking about:

▶ how we see ourselves

▶ how we judge what we do

▶ how we view the future

Our automatic thoughts echo our **core beliefs**. The more negative our core beliefs are, the more negative our automatic thoughts will be.

Unlovable Martin

www.davethompsonillustration.com

Martin had a core belief that no one loved him. This resulted in Marvin having lots of automatic thoughts that proved to him that this was right.

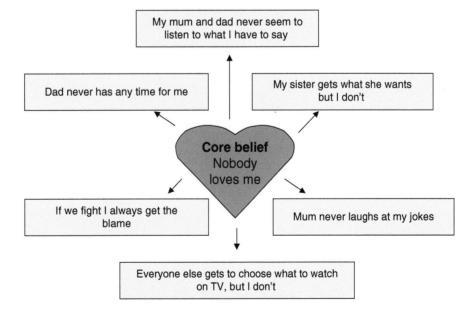

Think Good, Feel Good: A Cognitive Behavioural Therapy Workbook for Children and Young People, Second Edition. Paul Stallard.
© 2019 John Wiley & Sons Ltd. Published 2019 by John Wiley & Sons Ltd.
Companion website: www.wiley.com/go/thinkgoodfeelgood2e

We could probably see things in a slightly different way, but Martin saw a lot of these things as evidence that no one loved him.

Finding core beliefs

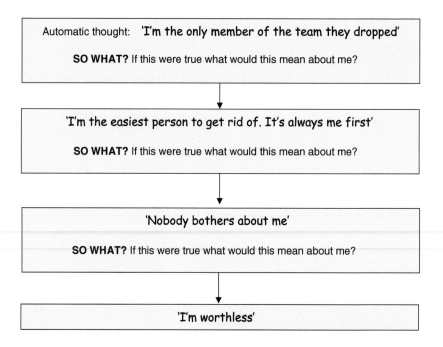

The **Thought Tracker** has found a useful way to help you find your core beliefs.

This is called the **SO WHAT?** method.

Take a negative thought and keep asking yourself '**SO WHAT? If this was true, what would this mean about me**'?

Keep repeating this question until you find your core belief.

Sally is dropped from the team

Sally felt really down after she was dropped from the netball team. She had lots of negative thoughts, so the **Thought Tracker** helped her to identify her core beliefs.

Automatic thought: 'I'm the only member of the team they dropped'

SO WHAT? If this were true what would this mean about me?

↓

'I'm the easiest person to get rid of. It's always me first'

SO WHAT? If this were true what would this mean about me?

↓

'Nobody bothers about me'

SO WHAT? If this were true what would this mean about me?

↓

'I'm worthless'

James gets poor marks

James received his examination marks and became very upset. Although he had got good marks, they didn't seem good enough to him. With the help of the **Thought Tracker**, James explored his thoughts and identified his core beliefs.

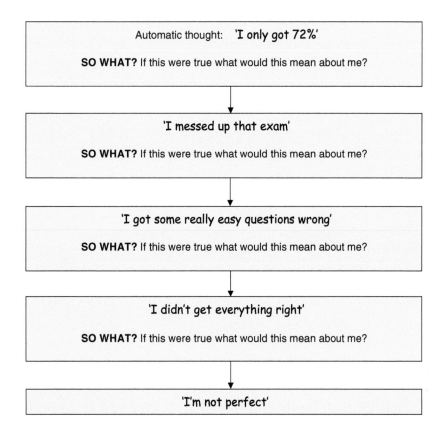

Identifying core beliefs can help you understand why you end up thinking the same way.

▷ Sally has a **core belief that she is worthless**. This helped Sally to understand why she was always putting herself down and devaluing her achievements.

▷ James has a **core belief that he must be perfect**. He tries to avoid attempting anything new or different in case he finds he can't do it.

Helpful Tips

Identifying core beliefs can help you understand why the same problems keep occurring

Challenging core beliefs

Once we have identified our core beliefs, the next step is to test them and check to see whether they really are true.

Core beliefs are like our automatic thoughts – we hear them and accept them as true without really questioning them. We need to ask ourselves the following questions.

▷ Are we seeing the whole story?

▷ Are we missing any evidence that would suggest that this belief is not true?

We need to look for evidence that **does not support** our core belief. No matter how small or unimportant, it may seem – **FIND IT**

Peter is bad

Peter had a core belief that he was a bad person. He thought that he always made people unhappy, always got into trouble, and was always being told off.

The **Thought Tracker** helped Peter to test this belief. For one day, Peter kept a diary of what happened in each of his lessons at school. Peter had to look for evidence that would question his core belief, so he wrote down whenever someone said something good or nice about him. After all, you can't be a bad person if people say good things about you.

At the end of the day, Peter's diary looked like this:

Maths   Teacher praised Peter for doing his homework.
English   Nothing said.
Science   Teacher made three positive comments about Peter's work and one
           comment about his positive attitude.
History   Nothing said.
English   Nothing said.
Friends   Peter was invited back to Richard's house after school.

At the end of the day, Peter looked at his diary. He hadn't got into trouble at all, some people had said good things about him, and Richard wanted to see him after school.

Although Peter saw these things, they were not strong enough to make him question his core belief. He dismissed what happened, saying 'It's not usually like that'.

The **Thought Tracker** helped again. Peter was caught in a **thinking trap** – he was being down on himself and was playing down anything positive that happened. The **Thought Tracker** suggested that Peter should keep the diary going for a week. This would check whether today had been a 'one-off' event or whether perhaps things were better than Peter realised.

Talk with someone

Because core beliefs are very strong you may, like Peter, find that they are difficult to challenge. This can lead you to reject any evidence that might suggest your core belief is not always right.

At these times, it can be useful to talk with someone else. Talk with a good friend or someone close to you and find out whether they see things the same way as you. Another person may provide new information or may highlight things that you find difficult to see or believe.

Remember!

We are very good at looking for and finding evidence that supports our core beliefs.

To find your core beliefs take a negative thought and keep asking yourself **SO WHAT?**

Keeping a diary or a list of evidence that **does not support** your core belief can help you check whether you are seeing the whole picture.

If you find this difficult, **talk with someone** else. You may be stuck in a thinking trap and be unable to see things differently. Someone else may be able to point out the things that you are overlooking.

Finding core beliefs

Take one of your most common negative thoughts and use the **SO WHAT** method to discover your core belief. Keep asking 'SO WHAT' until you find your core belief.

> **My thought:**
>
> **SO WHAT?** If this were true what would this mean about me?

SO WHAT? If this were true what would this mean about me?

SO WHAT? If this were true what would this mean about me?

SO WHAT? If this were true what would this mean about me?

SO WHAT? If this were true what would this mean about me?

My Core Belief

Are my beliefs always true?

Select one of your core beliefs and over the next week record **any evidence**, no matter how small, that would suggest that this core belief is **not always true**.

My core belief

Evidence that it is **not always true**.

Common beliefs

Use the Thermometer from Chapter 12 to rate how much you agree with each of the following statements.

It is important to be better than others at everything I do

Thought rating

Other people are better than me

Thought rating

No one loves or cares about me

Thought rating

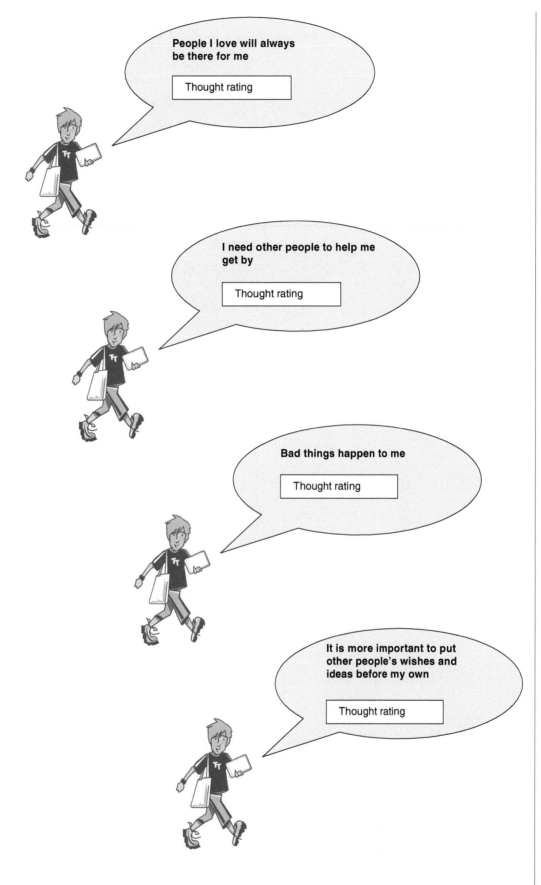

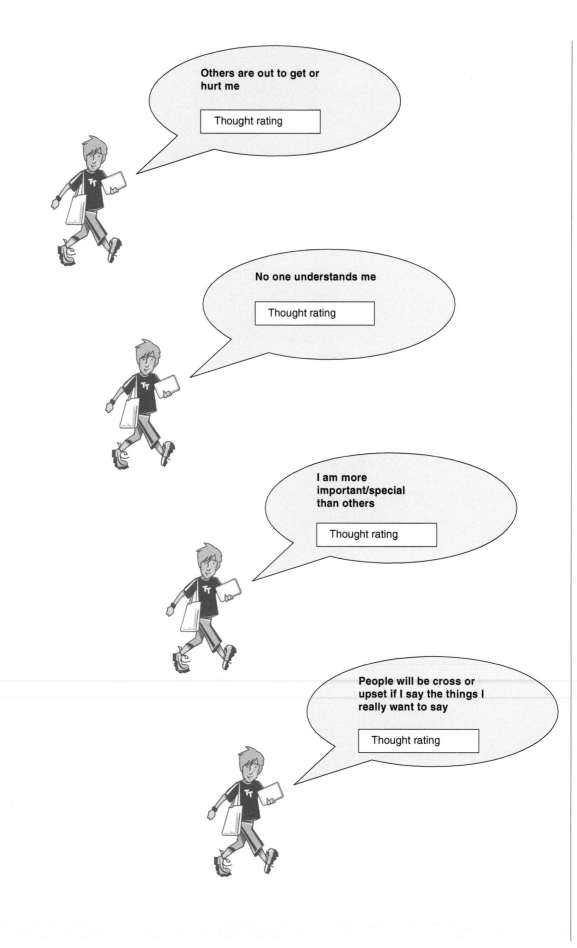

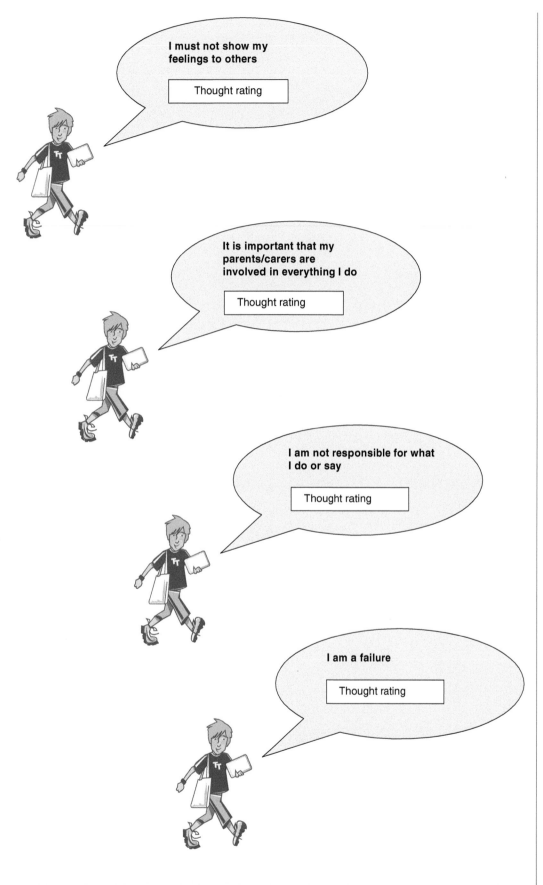

Controlling your thoughts

We spend a great deal of time listening to our thoughts. Some of these thoughts are negative and are about ourselves, what we do, and what we expect to happen in the future. As we have already found out, we accept many of these thoughts as true without really questioning them, particularly the negative ones. We then become trapped.

▶ The negative thoughts become louder.

▶ It becomes harder to turn down the volume and hear any other thoughts.

▶ The more we listen, the more unpleasant feelings we experience, and the less we end up doing.

Step back from your thoughts

We can learn to be less bothered by our thoughts by accepting them for what they are – passing thoughts. You can learn to develop a better relationship with your thoughts by stepping back from them. Let them come and go. Notice how one passes through another arrives. Just because you have these thoughts does not mean they are true. Don't argue or react to them. You may find that some of the exercises in Here and Now (Chapter 5) may help you to do this.

Helpful Tips

Don't get upset or bothered by your thoughts. Let them come and go, and don't react or argue with them.

Think Good, Feel Good: A Cognitive Behavioural Therapy Workbook for Children and Young People, Second Edition. Paul Stallard.
© 2019 John Wiley & Sons Ltd. Published 2019 by John Wiley & Sons Ltd.
Companion website: www.wiley.com/go/thinkgoodfeelgood2e

Refocus your attention

We have started to identify some of our unhelpful thoughts and to learn about the different types of thinking traps. Looking for new evidence to test these thoughts is important, and it will help us to check that our thinking is balanced.

For some people, negative automatic thoughts occur so often there just doesn't seem enough time in the day to check and challenge each one. Because they may occur so often, we need to find ways to stop them as soon as we notice them.

The **Thought Tracker** has some ideas to help you regain control of your thoughts. You may not always find them easy to use, and there will probably be times when you may be aware of your thoughts but feel unable to turn them off. Try not to worry about this. If these ideas work for some of the time, then they are useful, but remember, the more you practice, the better you will become.

Distraction

You may notice that in some situations, you often feel uncomfortable or have regular negative or unhelpful thoughts. At these times, you may want some short-term relief, and this is where **distraction** techniques may be helpful.

Distraction helps you to take your mind off of your negative thoughts and to control them by thinking about something else.

Helpful Tips

If you continue listening to your negative thoughts, they will become louder and take over.

The idea of distraction is to train yourself to keep your mind busy doing what you want it to do. You teach yourself to focus your thoughts on something else. Rather than listening to worrying or unhelpful thoughts, you learn to drown them out by getting your mind to do what you want it to do. There are different ways you can distract yourself.

Tigatelu/istock via Getty Images

Describe what you see

This involves describing to yourself in detail what you see. Try to do this as quickly as you can, and think about colours, shapes, size, smells, textures, and so forth.

■ Mary feels frightened

Mary often feels very frightened during her history lesson at school. She can remember a time when the teacher embarrassed her in front of her classmates. Mary still thinks about this incident, and it still scares her. When Mary starts to feel frightened, she worries more and often ends up thinking about how she is feeling, fearing that she will go red, and pass out.

Mary needs to regain control of her thoughts. She needs to think about what is going on around her, rather than concentrating on how she is feeling. The next time she felt frightened, Mary tried describing what she saw. Her description went like this:

I'm sitting in a class with about 15 other girls. My teacher, Mrs Evans, is standing at the front. She is wearing a black top, red crew-neck jumper, and a knee length black skirt. There is writing on the board – today's date, Wednesday 16, and tonight's homework which is to copy our rough work into our books. Next to me is Sally. She is wearing a white blouse, cuffs turned back, and a black skirt and tights. She has three books on her desk, all closed, and she is fiddling with her pencil.

By this stage, Mary was beginning to feel calmer. She had drowned out her worrying thoughts and had regained control. When she started to feel frightened again, Mary repeated this task until she felt calm and in control.

Mind games

At other times, you may want to occupy your thoughts by playing mind games. These are thinking puzzles which require you to concentrate on and puzzles such as the following:

▶ counting backwards from 123 in 9s'

▶ spelling the names of your family backwards

▶ naming the records of your favourite group

▶ naming all the players in your favourite sports team

Helpful Tips

The mind game has to be hard enough to challenge you, so don't make it too easy. The idea is that the task takes over and drowns out any unhelpful or negative thoughts you might be having.

Absorbing activities

Some people find that they can switch off and become totally absorbed in certain activities.

Reading, watching the television/video, playing an instrument, listening to the radio, or to music may be helpful.

The more you concentrate on what you are doing, the more you drown out any negative thoughts.

At those times, when you become aware that you are listening to your unhelpful negative thoughts, try one of the activities which you find helpful. For example

> Instead of lying in bed listening to your negative or unhelpful thoughts, put on your personal stereo and listen to some music.

> Instead of worrying whether your friend will call, read a book do some colouring, or do a puzzle.

The more you practice the easier you will find it to block out your negative thoughts.

Coping self-talk

Unhelpful thoughts often increase anxious or unhappy feelings. Instead of listening to them, try and change them by way of **coping self-talk.** This is a way of thinking that

> **Encourages you** to try rather than to give up or avoid things

> Helps you to feel **less anxious, sad, or angry**

> Helps you to **cope**

It can be very helpful to say your coping thoughts out loud to make sure that you hear them.

Coping self-talk is useful if you are preparing to do something that really worries you. At these difficult times, instead of listening to your doubts or worries, repeat your coping thoughts. These **recognise** how you are feeling, **motivate** you to try, and **remind** you that you will cope.

> Instead of listening to unhelpful thoughts like '*I can't do this*', try repeating some **coping thoughts** '*I am feeling worried, but I am not going to let my anxiety boss me around. I am going to do this*'.

> Instead of listening to unhelpful thoughts like *'This will go wrong and I will make a fool of myself'*, try repeating some **coping thoughts**, *'I am feeling scared, but I have done this before. I am going to do it now'*.

Helpful Tips

When planning to do something, don't listen to your unhelpful thoughts. Repeat out loud coping thoughts which encourage you to try and remind you that you will cope.

Positive self-talk

We are not always very good at praising ourselves for being successful. **Positive self-talk** is a way of helping us to take more notice of our achievements.

> Instead of thinking *'I've only answered 1 question – I'll never be able to finish all 10'*, use **positive self-talk** such as *'That's the first question done – now for the next one'*.

> Instead of thinking *'I don't talk very much when I am with my friends'*, use **positive self-talk** such as *'That was the first time I've ever spoken to Rory'*.

Helpful Tips

Positive self-talk helps you to recognise that although things may not be perfect, they may be better than you think.

Amy doesn't like going out

Amy becomes very anxious and fearful whenever she goes out of her house. She has lots of negative and unhelpful thoughts about what will happen, and these make her feel very anxious.

Amy decided to try coping and positive self-talk when she next went out. Instead of listening to her negative doubts and worries, she decided to think differently.

Before Amy went out she used her **coping self-talk.** Amy said to herself out loud, *'I am scared, but I am going to do this today'*; *'It will be alright'*; *'I have been out before, and everything was OK'*; *'I'm feeling relaxed. I'm in charge, and I will go out'*.

As Amy walked down the road, she used her **positive self-talk**, with comments such as *'That's good. I'm halfway there'*; *'I knew I could do it. It's going to be OK'*. Amy kept repeating these thoughts to herself until she returned home.

After Amy arrived home she remembered to congratulate herself and thought *'Well done'*; *'That wasn't so bad after all'*. She treated herself to a long, relaxing bubble bath.

Thought stopping

Sometimes, you will find that you are only able to stop your thoughts for a short time before they break through again. At these times, you could try some of the exercises in 'Here and Now' which can help you to step back from your thoughts.

Another method you could use to control your thoughts is **thought stopping**. As soon as you become aware of the thought, follow the steps below:

S. Hanusch/Shutterstock

▷ Immediately and loudly say **STOP.**

▷ Some people find it useful to emphasise this by banging the table or holding a chair or table tightly.

▷ Straight away think of your challenge to this negative thought and repeat it loudly to yourself.

Omar had to talk in school assembly

Omar had to talk during the school assembly about the project he had been working on. All the time he was waiting to talk, unhelpful thoughts were racing through his head:

'You're not going to do this right'; 'I'll go red and forget what to say'; 'Everyone will be looking at me'.

Omar had had enough. He was getting more and more anxious. He decided to use thought stopping. He said clearly and loudly to himself '**STOP**'. As soon as he said this, he challenged his negative thoughts and started to use his coping self-talk: *'This may not be easy, but I want to do this. It doesn't matter if I do go red, my teacher will help'.*

Omar repeated this to himself a few times and started to calm down.

Thought stopping will stop you from listening to the unhelpful thoughts tumbling around your head. Stop the unhelpful thoughts, and think how you will cope and be successful.

Turn the volume down

Another way of doing this is to imagine a CD player in your head that is playing your negative thoughts. Imagine what the CD player looks like and describe it to yourself in as much detail as possible.

▶ What does it look like?

▶ What size and colour is it?

▶ Where are the controls?

▶ How do you turn it on/off?

▶ How do you alter the volume?

The more you concentrate on your CD player, the clearer your picture will become. Once you have a good picture in your head imagine yourself changing the settings.

▶ As you turn the volume up, notice the sound become louder.

▶ As you turn the volume down, notice how the sound becomes quieter.

▶ As you turn the player off, notice how silent it becomes.

▶ As you turn the player on, notice how you start to hear the sound again.

Practice changing the controls. The more you practice, the easier it will become.

When you notice that you are listening to your unhelpful negative thoughts, imagine your CD player and turn the volume down or turn the CD player off.

Limit the time you worry

If you spend a lot of your time worrying, then it can be helpful to put some limits around your worries. Rather than worrying throughout the day make a regular 15-minute time each day to focus on your worries (e.g. 5.00–5.15). During this time, you can worry about whatever you want.

▶ During the day, if you notice yourself worrying, write your worries down and focus your attention on something else.

▶ At worry time, look through your list and sort them out.

▶ You will notice that some worries will have disappeared and are no longer important or bother you.

▶ Other worries might be about real events which you can do something about. The problem-solving ideas in Chapter 15 can help you work out what you can do.

▶ Others will be the 'what if' type of worries – imaginary worries which you can do nothing about. Learn to accept that you won't always know what will happen and enjoy what is happening here and now.

Helpful Tips

Setting a worry time each day can help you spend less time worrying. You will discover that you don't need to spend all day worrying

Test them

Sometimes, it is useful to test your thoughts and beliefs by setting up experiments to find out whether what you expect actually happens. This is particularly useful if you often fall into the predicting failure trap.

Julie's schoolwork

Julie did not believe that she was good at any of her school subjects. She thought that she always got her work wrong. To test this belief, Julie wrote down the results of her next 10 homework assignments.

Core Belief: I'm not clever

Automatic thoughts: I always get my homework wrong. I can't do this.

Test : The marks I get for my next 10 homework assignments.

What I expect to happen (my prediction): To get poor marks (less than 6/10) for all of my homework assignments

What happened?

1 English 3/10. You need to write more, Julie, and make sure that you answer the question.

2 Maths 7/10. Well done, Julie. Good work.

3 Maths 7/10. Keep it up, Julie.

4 English 4/10. Answer the questions please, Julie.

5 Geography 6/10. Nice map.

6 Art 9/10. Excellent work.

7 English 2/10. Can you please see me, Julie. This is not good enough.

8 History 5/10. Not your best work.

9 Maths 8/10. Good work.

10 English 4/10. Check your spelling and please write more neatly.

This test showed that Julie was having a problem with her English. As Julie had thought, she was getting poor marks, and she wasn't answering the questions. Her history teacher also thought she could do better, **BUT** the marks Julie obtained for her other five homework assignments in maths, art, and geography were good. This helped Julie to find a more balanced way of thinking about her schoolwork.

Throw them away

Thoughts tumble around inside our heads:

▶ No one hears them.

▶ No one questions them.

Sometimes, it is useful to empty our heads and clear our thoughts away.

At the end of the day, write down your negative unhelpful thoughts on a piece of paper. If you want, you can type them on your computer.

Think of them all and write them all down.

Once you have finished, press the delete button or scrunch up your paper tightly and put it in the bin.

Ruslan Gilyazov/123RF

davib/Shutterstock

Remember!

▷ There are different ways in which you can take control of and challenge your unhelpful thoughts.

▷ You will probably need to use a range of methods.

▷ The method that you choose will not always be successful.

▷ The more you practice, the easier it will become, so stick with it.

Test your thoughts and beliefs

If you often fall into the **predicting failure** thinking trap, it can be useful to test your thoughts and beliefs. Set up an experiment to find out whether what you expect actually happens.

1 What is the negative belief/thought that you hear most often?

2 Use the thermometer from Chapter 12 to rate how strongly you believe this thought.

3 What experiment could you set up to test whether this is true?

4 When will you carry out your test?

5 If your belief/thoughts were true, what do you predict would happen?

6 What did happen?

7 Use the thermometer to rate how strongly you now believe this thought.

The thought challenger

With the help of the Thought Tracker identify the unhelpful or negative thoughts that you hear most often.

My most common unhelpful thought is

Look at **all** the evidence. What would be a more balanced thought?

A more balanced thought is

Whenever you notice this unhelpful thought:

1 Say **STOP** to yourself

2 Repeat your balanced thought two or three times – this will help to turn down the volume of the unhelpful thought.

Don't just listen to your unhelpful thoughts. Challenge them and turn down the volume.

Looking for the positive

We always seem to notice the things that aren't quite right, but we are not very good at noticing the positive or good things that happen.

Each night before you go to bed, think of three things that have happened that have made you feel good. These could be anything such as

▶ nice thoughts about yourself

▶ positive thoughts about what you have done or achieved

▶ activities that have made you feel good

▶ things others have said that made you feel good

Each day write down three positive things. If you can't think of three good things, then ask someone to help.

Good things that happen

Watching the list grow will help you realise that positive things do happen to you.

THINK GOOD, FEEL GOOD

Positive self-talk

We are not very good at recognising our achievements. Often, we think about the things that have gone wrong or which aren't quite right.

Positive self-talk focuses on being successful.

You may find this difficult at first, so don't worry. The more you practice, the easier it will become.

Write down some of your unhelpful thoughts.

Write down the positive and helpful things that will help you to be successful.

What would be your positive and helpful self-talk?

Use positive self-talk to find your achievements and to focus on being successful.

Coping self-talk

Some of our thoughts are not helpful. In fact, they make us feel more anxious or worried. These thoughts make us think that things will go wrong and make us expect that bad things will happen. Learning to identify and replace these thoughts with coping self-talk will help you to feel better.

Think about a situation or event that makes you feel anxious or unpleasant. When you are in this situation, write down or draw a picture of the thoughts that race through your mind. Once you have done this, think about how you can challenge these thoughts with coping self-talk.

The situation that makes me feel anxious or worried is

The thoughts that make me feel anxious are

My coping self-talk which will help me to cope is

The next time you are in that situation, use coping self-talk to help you feel better.

The worry safe

Sometimes, it is difficult to stop worrying and to turn off the thoughts that are going around in our heads.

When this happens, it may be useful to empty your head. Write or draw these thoughts on a piece of paper and lock them away.

dedMazay/Shutterstock

▶ Find a box and make your own worry safe. Paint and colour it as you like and choose a place to keep it.

▶ When you find that you can't stop your worries, find some paper and draw them or write them down.

▶ Once you have finished, lock them away in your worry safe.

▶ At the end of the week, unlock your safe, and talk about your worries with mum, dad, or someone you trust.

**Once your worries are in the safe, they will find
it harder to trouble you.**

Turn the CD off

Sometimes, you may hear the same worries or unhelpful thoughts over and over again. It is like listening to a CD that is being played in your head.

▷ The CD plays the same thoughts over and over again.

▷ The CD never gets changed.

▷ At these times, it is useful to learn how to stop or turn the volume down on your CD player.

Step 1: Imagine your CD player

▷ Imagine a picture of a CD player in your head.

▷ You may find that looking at a real CD player can help you to make a good picture.

▷ Really look at the CD player and see how you turn it on and off, where you put the CD, and how you change the volume.

Step 2: Imagine stopping the CD

▷ Think of this picture and imagine yourself turning the CD player off.

▷ Really concentrate on the 'off' switch and as you touch the button notice how your unhelpful thoughts stop.

▷ Practice turning your CD player on and off, and notice how the 'off' switch stops your negative thoughts.

Remember that the more your practice, the easier it will become.

Worry time

Limit the amount of time you spend worrying by creating a daily worry time.
Write down below any worries that happen during the day.

Worries that are bothering me:

During worry time, sort your worries into those you can do something about
and those you can't.

Worries I can do something about here and now. Write your plan next to
each worry

Worries I can do nothing about

**Solve the worries you can do something about and accept those that you
have no control over.**

Practice being successful

When faced with new or difficult challenges, we often think that we shall not be successful. We are very good at predicting failure and thinking that things will go wrong.

Thinking like this will make us feel anxious and reluctant to try anything new or challenging. Try to imagine a picture of your challenge, but this time change the ending so that you are successful.

Step 1: Imagine your challenge

Make your picture as real as possible and describe your challenge in plenty of detail. Think about:

▶ who will be there

▶ the time of day

▶ what you are wearing

▶ the colours, smells, and sounds.

Step 2: Talk yourself through your challenge

Now think about what will happen and imagine being successful.

▶ What will you do?

▶ What will you say?

▶ What will the other people do?

▶ What will they say?

▶ What will happen?

Practicing a few times will help you to prepare yourself, and may help you to recognise that although it might be difficult, you can be successful.

Thought stopping

Sometimes, the same unhelpful thoughts go round and round in our heads. The more we hear, them the more we

▷ believe them

▷ look for evidence that supports them.

When we check them out, we often find that we are only seeing part of the picture – usually, the negative part. It is important to try and stop these unhelpful thoughts.

A useful way of doing this is to wear an elastic band on your wrist.

▷ When you notice that you are listening to the same unhelpful thoughts snap the elastic band.

The elastic band will hurt a little, but this will probably take your mind of those unhelpful thoughts.

How you feel

Each day you will probably notice a range of different feelings. For example, you could

▶ Wake up feeling **anxious** about going to school

▶ Feel **happy** on the school bus talking with friends

▶ Feel **angry** when your friend forgets to bring the DVD you wanted to borrow

▶ Feel **stressed** completing your homework

▶ Feel **relaxed** watching TV

You will find

▶ that some of these feelings will only last a **short time**.

▶ others will go **on and on**.

▶ some will be so **weak** that you may not even notice them.

▶ others will be **very strong** and seem to take over.

Helpful Tips

Our first job is to find out more about the type of feelings that you have. This is not always easy because

▶ we are not always very good at identifying our feelings.

▶ we often wrap all our feelings up together under one label.

To help you discover your feelings you may need the help of the **Feelings Finder**. The **Feelings Finder** can help you to discover:

▶ What feelings you have

▶ What feelings are the strongest

▶ Where you are most likely to have these feelings

▶ What thoughts go with these feelings

What feelings do I have?

Learning to identify your feelings is important. Identifying them may help you learn how to control them. For example, breathing exercises may help with feelings of anxiety or worry, but not with feelings of sadness.

Three of the strongest and most common unpleasant feelings are stress, unhappiness, and anger.

Stress

When people feel stressed or wound up, they notice a number of different symptoms. The signs of stress vary from one person to another but may include

▶ feeling sick

▶ butterflies in the stomach

▶ shortness of breath

▶ sweating

▶ legs feeling heavy or like jelly

▶ going red in the face

▶ feeling light-headed

▶ fainting

▶ aching muscles

▶ your mind going blank

▶ difficulty making decisions

Unhappiness

Everyone feels unhappy at some time or another, but for some this feeling takes over their life, and they end up feeling very depressed. They might find themselves

- regularly tearful

- crying for no clear reason or over small things

- waking up early in the morning

- having difficulty in falling asleep at night

- feeling constantly tired and lacking in energy

- comfort eating or losing their appetite

- having difficulty in concentrating

- losing interest in things they use to enjoy

- going out less often

Because these feelings produce some very strong physical reactions people sometimes end up thinking that they are ill or unwell. These symptoms then become the reason why they stop or avoid doing things.

- *'I'm feeling hot and sick so I can't go to school'.*

These physical reactions are very real, but you may not be unwell. It may be part of a trap where your negative thoughts create these symptoms. If you are unsure or want some reassurance, then check this out by talking with your doctor.

Anger

Anger is a very common feeling and can be expressed in many different ways:

- shouting, yelling, and screaming

- swearing and threatening

- throwing things

- breaking things

- slamming doors

- hitting, kicking, and fighting

- wanting to harm oneself

Feelings and what you do

Feelings don't just suddenly happen. There is usually something that triggers them. How you feel will be affected by what you do and what you think.

The **Feelings Finder** has helped people to learn that they have different feelings in **different places**,

▶ At school, you may feel **anxious**

▶ At home, you may feel **relaxed**

▶ In town, you may feel **worried**

You will notice different feelings when you engage in different **activities**.

▶ When watching TV, you may feel **calm**.

▶ When talking with people, you may feel **anxious**.

▶ When doing Maths, you may feel **happy**.

▶ When playing sport, you may feel **tense**.

You will also notice that you have different feelings with different **people**.

▶ With your dad, you may feel **angry**.

▶ With your best friend, you may feel **relaxed** and confident.

▶ With your teacher, you may feel **happy**.

▶ With your sister, you may feel **stressed**.

Feelings and what you think

The way we think creates feelings.

▶ If you **think** that you have no friends, you may **feel sad**.

▶ If you **think** that you are disliked, you may **feel worried**.

▶ If you **think** that you did well with your homework, you may **feel pleased**.

Putting it together

If you put it all together, you will probably start to notice a pattern.

What you do	How you feel	What you think
At home, alone	Sad	I've got no friends
Go out with Jim	Happy	We always have a laugh together
Go to school	Stressed	I just can't keep up with my work
Go shopping for clothes	Angry	I can never find anything that looks good on me
Have a bath	Relaxed, calm	It's nice lying here

Remember!

How we feel depends on what we do and what we think.

Try and identify the different feelings that you have.

Check whether your strongest feelings are linked to particular thoughts or what you do.

Thoughts and feelings

Write down three of your thoughts that make you feel good and three that make you feel unpleasant:

Thoughts that make me **feel good:**

1.

2.

3.

Thoughts that make me **feel unpleasant:**

1.

2.

3.

What you do and how you feel

Write down three activities that make you feel good and three that make you feel unpleasant:

Activities that make me **feel good**:

1.

2.

3.

Activities that make me **feel unpleasant**:

1.

2.

3.

Feelings word search

Can you find these feelings the **Feelings Finder** has hidden?

Happy	Angry	Afraid	Scared
Grumpy	Tense	Anxious	Unhappy
Worried	Wound up	Sad	Uptight
Depressed	Calm	Tearful	Excited
Relaxed	Guilty	Ashamed	Insecure
Frightened	Nervous	Hurt	Confused
Upset	Mad		

N	H	C	K	H	G	F	D	S	E	W	T	Y	U	N	F	C
H	A	N	G	R	Y	M	M	L	Q	U	P	T	I	G	H	T
C	P	W	R	K	F	B	D	I	A	N	G	F	F	X	Z	E
O	P	G	U	I	L	T	Y	N	P	H	M	N	N	G	F	A
N	Y	T	M	T	F	X	Z	S	C	A	R	E	D	S	W	R
F	E	Y	P	V	T	Y	D	E	S	P	I	R	Q	E	R	F
U	F	H	Y	N	E	L	P	C	T	P	R	V	G	J	K	U
S	D	F	G	H	N	P	R	U	G	Y	F	O	V	B	N	L
E	A	J	H	J	S	A	D	R	H	I	R	U	G	H	F	W
D	N	N	U	K	E	Y	E	E	J	K	G	S	M	K	R	D
F	X	B	R	A	D	Y	P	S	K	C	F	F	A	J	I	F
W	I	V	T	F	R	H	R	E	L	A	X	E	D	H	G	G
H	O	C	B	R	F	H	E	D	X	L	W	Q	U	L	H	H
J	U	U	B	A	V	A	S	H	A	M	E	D	P	O	T	Y
K	S	P	N	I	V	B	S	H	S	Z	S	X	T	Y	E	T
M	D	S	W	D	N	V	E	X	C	I	T	E	D	M	N	R
N	F	E	P	V	U	L	D	K	J	L	A	Z	P	L	E	Y
R	G	T	D	C	Q	P	O	W	O	R	R	I	E	D	D	J

What are your most common feelings?

What feeling goes where?

We have different feelings in different places. Use a different colour and draw a line from each place to the feeling that best describes how you feel.

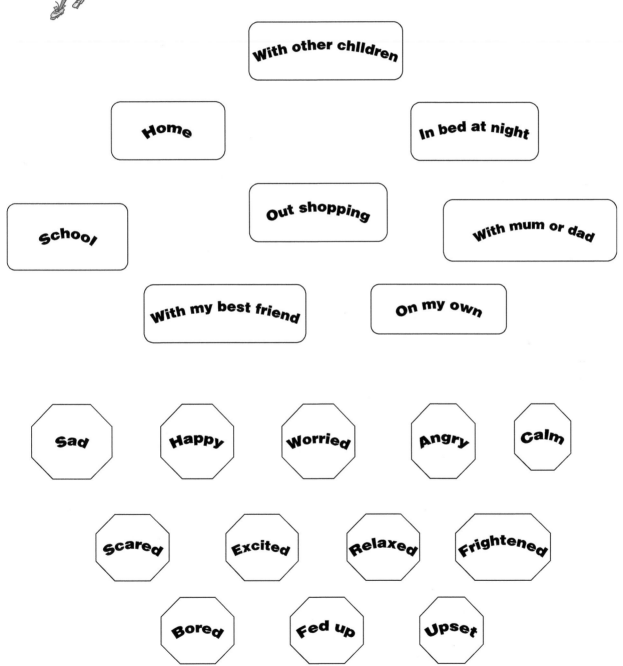

My feelings

Think about all the different feelings you have (pleasant and unpleasant) and draw or write them down on a piece of paper.

▶ Choose a coloured pen or pencil for each feeling (you could choose something like red for happy, blue, for sad, etc.).

▶ Use these colours and draw your feelings on the picture below.

▶ Try and show how much you have of each feeling.

What happens when I feel sad?

Think about something that made you feel really sad and unhappy. How would someone else know that you felt like this?

Phon Promwisate/Shutterstock

What does you face look like when you are sad?

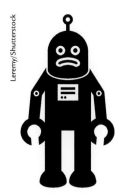

Leremy/Shutterstock

How does your body show that you are unhappy?

Kakigori Studio/Shutterstock

How do you behave when you are unhappy?

How much of the time do you feel unhappy?

Never									All the time
1	2	3	4	5	6	7	8	9	10

What happens when I feel angry?

Think about something that made you feel really cross and angry. How would someone know that you felt like this?

What does you face look like when you are angry?

How does your body show that you are angry?

How do you behave when you are angry?

How much of the time do you feel angry?

Never									All the time
1	2	3	4	5	6	7	8	9	10

What happens when I feel anxious?

Think about something that made you feel really anxious or uptight. How would someone else know that you felt like this?

Phon Promwisate/Shutterstock

What does you face look like when you are anxious or uptight?

Leremy/Shutterstock

How does your body show that you are anxious or uptight?

danbailey/istock via Getty Images

How do you behave when you are anxious or uptight?

How much of the time do you feel anxious or uptight?

Never									All the time
1	2	3	4	5	6	7	8	9	10

What happens when I feel happy?

Think about something that made you feel really happy. How would someone else know that you felt like this?

What does you face look like when you are happy?

How does your body show that you are happy?

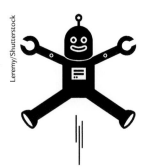

How do you behave when you are happy?

How much of the time do you feel happy?

Never									All the time
1	2	3	4	5	6	7	8	9	10

Feelings and places

Think about all your different feelings and write them on sheets of paper.

Make a list of the main places, people, and activities in your life. The list might include some of these:

1 Mum

2 Dad

3 Grandparents

4 Best friend

5 Other children

6 School

7 Home

8 Leisure/activity club

9 Playing sport, game, and reading a book

10 In bed at night

11 Watching TV

12 Doing schoolwork

13 Going somewhere new

14 Going to school

15 Being with friends

Choose which feelings go with each of the above.

What gives you the **most pleasant feelings?**

What gives you the **most unpleasant feelings?**

The thermometer

Chose a number between 1 and 10 to show how strong your feelings or thoughts are.

10 Very strong

9

8

7 Fairly strong

6

5

4 Weak

3

2

1 Very weak

CHAPTER THIRTEEN

Controlling your feelings

www.davethompsonillustration.com

The **Feeling Finder** has helped us to discover that the places we go to or the things we do may sometimes produce strong feelings. For example, you may notice that you

▷ feel **anxious** when you **go out**

▷ feel **calm** and safe at **home**

▷ feel **worried** when **with others**

▷ feel **relaxed** and happy **on your own**

We try to do things or go to places that give us pleasant feelings, and we try to avoid those that make us feel unpleasant.

This seems to make sense. After all, none of us want to feel unpleasant for most of the day.

But sometimes your feelings take over and **stop or limit** what you really want to do.

▷ You may **want** to go out, but because you feel so anxious you **feel unable** to go.

▷ You may **want** to be with friends, but because you feel so worried you **feel unable** to see them.

▷ You may **want** to call up a friend, but because you feel so unhappy you **feel unable** to do it.

At these times, the way you feel is stopping or preventing you from doing those things that you really want to. Learning how to control your feelings will help break down these barriers.

Think Good, Feel Good: A Cognitive Behavioural Therapy Workbook for Children and Young People, Second Edition. Paul Stallard.
© 2019 John Wiley & Sons Ltd. Published 2019 by John Wiley & Sons Ltd.
Companion website: www.wiley.com/go/thinkgoodfeelgood2e

Helpful Tips

If you feel unpleasant, do something to make yourself feel better.

Learn to relax

There are different ways in which you can learn to relax. Some methods will take you through a series of physical exercises to tense and then relax each of the large muscle groups in your body. Others teach you to imagine relaxing pictures in your mind, and these calming pictures will help you feel more pleasant. It is important to remember the following points:

▶ There is no **one way** of relaxing.

▶ People find **different methods** useful at different times.

▶ It is important to **find what works for you**.

Physical relaxation

This method usually takes about 10 minutes and is very useful if you feel constantly tense or wound-up. Using a series of short exercises, all of the major muscle groups in your body are tensed for about five seconds and then relaxed.

Concentrate on what the muscles feel like when they are tensed and what they feel like when they are relaxed. You will find that some parts of your body will be tenser than others, so try to find the very tense areas.

By the end of the session you should feel completely relaxed, so enjoy this pleasant feeling. A number of people like to do these exercises before they go to bed. It does not matter if you fall asleep. Like everything else, the more you practice the better and faster you will become at relaxing.

There are various CDs you can buy that will teach you how to relax. Choose one you like and find restful. Before you start remember:

- Choose somewhere warm and quiet.

- Sit in a comfortable chair or lie on your bed.

- Choose a time when you will not be interrupted.

- Tense your muscles just enough to notice what if feels like. Don't overdo it.

- Tense your muscles for about three to five seconds.

- Tense each muscle group twice.

- After you have tensed a muscle try not to move it again.

reLAXatIOn If you can't find a CD, then try the following exercises.

- Start by taking five deep breaths. Slowly breathe in through your nose and out through your mouth.

- Now concentrate on your feet and curl up your toes. Scrunch them up, count to five, and release them. Notice the difference between tension and relaxation. Tense them again.

- Move your attention to your legs and tense your muscles by pushing your toes towards your knees. Count to five and release the tension.

- Tense your thighs by pushing the back of your legs against the chair or bed.

- Move to your stomach and tense this by sucking in your stomach and pushing your belly button towards your spine.

- Focus on your arms and hands and tense them by making a tight fist and curling your arms up towards your shoulders.

- Tense your back by arching your spine and pushing your shoulder blades together. Count to five, relax, and notice the difference between tension and relaxation.

- Focus on your neck and shoulders and push your shoulders up towards your ears.

- Now tense your chin and jaw by clenching your teeth and pushing your chin down towards your chest.

- Finally, tense the rest of the muscles in your face by closing your eyes and pressing your lips together tightly and screwing up you face.

- As you release each muscle notice the tension fade away.

- Return your attention to your breathing and enjoy this relaxed feeling.

Try building these exercises into your daily routine. If you did this before bed, it might help you to sleep better.

Quick relaxation

There may be times when you don't have time to tense and relax each of your muscles. A quicker way of doing this is to tense each of the major muscle groups together.

▶ **Arms and hands**: Clench your fists and push your arms straight out in front of you.

▶ **Legs and feet**: Push your toes downwards, gently raise your legs, and stretch them out in front of you.

▶ **Stomach**: Push out your tummy muscles, take a breath and hold it.

▶ **Shoulders**: Scrunch up your shoulders.

▶ **Neck**: Push your head back against the chair or bed.

▶ **Face**: Screw up your face, squeeze your eyes tight, and push your lips together.

Make a time each day to relax. It doesn't take long, and it can help you to feel relaxed.

Physical exercise

Some people find that **physical exercise** is as effective as systematically tensing and relaxing their muscles. After all, physical exercise does exactly the same thing – it tenses and relaxes your muscles.

A good run, quick walk, or swim can help you to get rid of any angry or anxious feelings.

If physical exercise works for you, then use it. It may be particularly useful to try at those times when you notice strong unpleasant feelings.

4-5-6 breathing

There are times when you may suddenly start to become tense or angry, and on these occasions, you won't have time to go through the relaxation exercises.

4-5-6 breathing is a quick method in which you concentrate and gain control of your breathing. You can use this method anywhere, and often people don't even notice what you are doing.

PaintDoor/Shutterstock

> Breathe in slowly through your nose to the count of 4.

> Hold the breath for five seconds.

> Slowly breathe out through your mouth to the count of 6. As you breathe say to yourself 'relax'.

> Repeat this three or four times until you feel calmer.

Helpful Tips

4-5-6 breathing is quick and easy to do. You can do this anywhere and no one will know what you are doing.

Your calming place

With this method you make yourself feel more pleasant by imagining a special place that makes you feel relaxed, calm, and happy.

Think about your special place. It could be somewhere you have been or an imaginary place. To create a good image find a photograph or draw a picture of your calming place. Try and make the picture as real as you can, and think about:

▶ What you **see** – the colours of the sky, the shape of the rocks, the pattern of the tree bark

▶ What you **hear** – the noise of the waves crashing on the beach, wind blowing in the trees

▶ What you **feel** – the wind blowing gently in your hair, the sun warming your face

▶ What you **smell** – the smell of the sea or the scent of pine forests

▶ What you **taste** – sweet ice cream or salty water in our mouth

 Helpful Tips — Practice imagining your relaxing place, and if you start to feel unpleasant, then try turning the picture on. Really, concentrate hard on your calming place and see if it helps you to relax.

Relaxing activities

There will probably be some things that you enjoy doing and which make you feel good. Examples of these might include

▶ reading a book

▶ watching TV

▶ listening to music

▶ taking the dog for a walk

If a particular activity makes you feel good, then try doing it when you notice unpleasant feelings. You may only be able to do this at certain times, but if you are

▶ sitting around on your own worrying about tomorrow, try reading a book

▶ sitting in your bedroom feeling unhappy, try watching TV

▶ lying in bed feeling uptight because you can't sleep, try listening to some music

▶ feeling angry, then take the dog for a walk

 Helpful Tips — Find out what works for you. If you feel unpleasant, try doing something to make yourself feel better.

Stop the build-up

Sometimes, we are aware of our feelings, but often, we leave it too late to do something about them. At these times, our feelings become too strong and no matter what we do, we just can't seem to regain control. We need to learn to identify these times so that we can try to control our feelings **BEFORE** they get too strong.

Jimmy's temper

Jimmy often felt very angry and became very wound up. This seemed to happen very quickly, and when he lost his temper, it took him a long time to calm down afterwards.

He travelled up the anger escalator very quickly, and before he could stop, Jimmy had exploded. The **Feeling Finder** tried to help Jimmy gain more control over his angry feelings. The **Feeling Finder** suggested that they should draw an anger volcano to help Jimmy to discover what happens as he becomes angry.

Hit them

Swear, Red Face, Mind Blank

Clench Fists, Grit Teeth, Angry Face, Threaten

Seems like a dream
Watching myself from above

Thoughts: "Stop It" . "I'm going to hit you"
Feels hot and starts to sweat.

Thoughts: "You're trying to wind me up"
Normal Voice & Volume, Feel Calm

Once Jimmy became aware of his anger build-up, the next stage was to learn how **to bail out** at an early stage and stop himself from exploding.

Jimmy was able to do this by imagining the last time he lost his temper. He imagined the picture as clearly as he could, but this time he changed the ending.

- Jimmy imagined himself **bailing out** before he lost his temper.
- He imagined himself walking away.
- He imagined the look of disappointment on the faces of the others who were teasing him.
- He imagined how pleased with himself he felt.
- He practised listening to the taunts of the other children and staying calm.

Jimmy practised every day. He was practicing a different ending, so he was better prepared, and this helped him to cope with the teasing the next time it happened.

There are lots of different things you can do to help you feel better:

- Choose those methods that feel right for you.
- Remember they won't always work, but do stick with it.
- The more you practice, the more likely they will help.

Remember!

The feeling strong room

We all have unpleasant feelings, but sometimes these feelings become very strong and are difficult to get rid of. They could make you feel very angry, sad, or frightened.

When you feel very unpleasant, you may want to try locking these feelings away somewhere safe so that they do not bother you so much.

▷ Find a box, make it into your '**strong room**' and decorate it as you wish.

▷ When you feel very unpleasant, get some paper and write or draw your feelings.

▷ Think about what is making you feel like this and write about or draw a picture of this too.

▷ Once you have finished, put these feelings away in the 'strong room'.

▷ At the end of the week, open your box and talk about your feelings with mum, dad, or someone you trust.

Putting your unpleasant feelings away in a strong room may help you to feel better.

The anger volcano

Think about how your body feels when you are calm, and how it feels when you are angry. Plot the changes you notice as you become angrier onto your Anger Volcano.

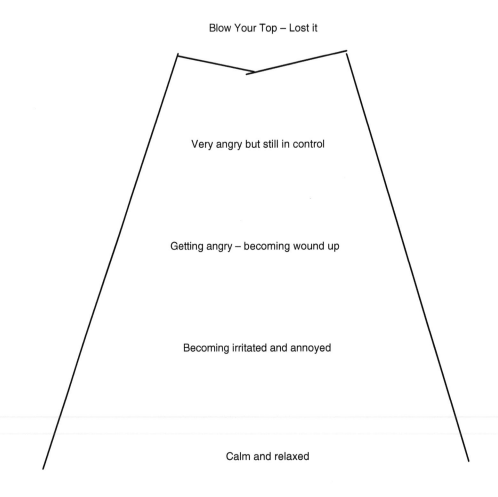

Blow Your Top – Lost it

Very angry but still in control

Getting angry – becoming wound up

Becoming irritated and annoyed

Calm and relaxed

Understanding how your anger builds up can help you learn to control it.

Learn to relax

For younger children, learning to relax can be made fun.

Muscles can be stretched and relaxed by playing a game such as 'Simon Says', in which the child is asked to do the following:

▷ March straight and upright around the room

▷ Run on the spot

▷ Pretend that their arms are branches of a tree by waving them above their head

▷ Screw up their face to look like a scary monster

▷ Stretch up to the sky and be as tall as possible

▷ Roll up tightly to become as small as possible

After the child has stretched their muscles, the final stage is to tell them to calm down and relax. Ask them to pretend to be a big heavy animal and to move around the room very slowly. Move as quietly and as slowly as possible. Finally, ask them to be 'sleeping lions' and lie on the floor as still and quiet as possible for a couple of minutes.

My calming place

A useful way of relaxing is to imagine your calming place. This can be a real place you have been to or somewhere you have created in your dreams.

You will need to practice this. The more you practice, the easier you will find it to imagine your picture, and the quicker you will become calm.

▷ Draw or find a picture of your calming place.

▷ Choose a quiet time when you will not be disturbed.

▷ Shut your eyes and imagine your calming place.

▷ Really concentrate and make it as detailed as possible.

▷ Think about the colours, shapes, and size of things.

▷ Listen for any sounds – seagulls calling, leaves rustling, waves crashing on the sand.

▷ Notice any smells – the smell of pine trees or the smell of the sea.

▷ Enjoy any tastes – salty water in your mouth or soft sweet ice cream.

▷ Imagine the sun warming your face.

▷ As you think of your picture, notice how calm and relaxed you have become.

▷ Enjoy this feeling for a few minutes.

When you feel yourself becoming stressed, think of your calming picture.

My relaxing activities

Fill in the thought bubbles by writing or drawing the things that help you to relax and feel calm.

Changing your behaviour

The **Thought Tracker** has helped us discover that sometimes we have negative and unhelpful thoughts. We think that things will be difficult. We expect and predict the worse. Sometimes it is hard to see anything positive.

The **Feeling Finder** has helped us understand that these thoughts may make us feel uncomfortable. When we feel like this, we try and find ways to make ourselves feel better.

Go-Getter can help us understand that the ways we make ourselves feel better are not always helpful. We might

▷ **avoid** situations that we think will be difficult

▷ **withdraw** and stay where we feel safe

▷ **stop** doing things that might make us feel unpleasant

This usually brings some immediate relief, but over time, you will probably feel worse. As you do less, you may find yourself feeling more and more down. Anything new needs an even greater effort, and it becomes harder to tackle any new challenges. Strong unpleasant feelings flood back as you feel cross and disappointed with yourself.

And so it goes on . . .

and on . . .

and on . . .

You need to get out of this trap and to regain control of your life. Get busy and push yourself to do things.

Think Good, Feel Good: A Cognitive Behavioural Therapy Workbook for Children and Young People, Second Edition. Paul Stallard.
© 2019 John Wiley & Sons Ltd. Published 2019 by John Wiley & Sons Ltd.
Companion website: www.wiley.com/go/thinkgoodfeelgood2e

Being busy is helpful

As you become busier, you will start to notice a number of benefits.

▶ **You feel better**
Becoming more active means you have less time to notice any unpleasant feelings or to listen to any negative thoughts. You will start to feel better.

▶ **You feel more in control**
Instead of being bossed around by your thoughts and feelings, you can regain control of your life and do the things you want to do.

▶ **You feel less tired**
Doing nothing is very tiring. You will feel very lethargic and exhausted. Although it sounds silly, the more active you become, the less tired you feel.

▶ **You want to do more**
The hardest thing is to get started. Once you become active, you will want to do more. Quite simply, the more you do, the more you feel like doing.

▶ **Your thinking becomes clearer**
Doing nothing makes you feel sluggish both mentally and physically. Activity sharpens up your thinking.

Have more fun

The first, and the hardest job, is to get going. **Go-Getter** has found that a useful way is to increase fun and enjoyable activities. Set yourself targets to increase the number of fun activities that you do each day or week. Make a **list** of the things that you:

▶ enjoy

▶ would like to do

▶ you used to enjoy doing but have now stopped

These don't have to cost money and could be

Social activities where you do things with other people. For example, you could

▶ go shopping with your sister

▶ go to the cinema with your friend

- eat with your family
- hang out with a friend

Physical activities where you become physically active by engaging in activities such as

- running
- dancing
- swimming
- a work out
- taking the dog for a walk
- sorting out your bedroom

Activities **you really enjoy** such as

- gaming
- cooking
- listening to music
- reading
- watching a DVD

Activities that give you a **sense of achievement and pride** like

- drawing
- playing an instrument
- fixing your bike
- sorting out your clothes
- completing a puzzle

From your list, decide on **one or two activities** you will do each week. Choose a day, set a time, and do it. Gradually, build more fun activities into your life.

Remember, don't try and do too much. The idea is to be successful, so set yourself small targets. It is better to set a target like playing your guitar once for five minutes rather than practicing for an hour.

Don't expect the activities to be as much fun as they used to be. It may take time for your sense of enjoyment to return.

> **Helpful Tips**
>
> Think about what you have achieved and make time to tell yourself how well you have done. After all, you deserve it.

Map how you feel and what you do

There will probably be certain times during the day/week when you are more likely to notice strong pleasant or unpleasant feelings. It may be useful to find out whether there are any patterns or particularly difficult times.

A useful way of doing this is to keep a diary.

Write down what you are doing and how you feel each hour. Use the Thermometer from Chapter 12 to rate how strong your feelings are.

At the end of the week, look at the diary, and see if there are any particularly bad/good times, and whether any activity made you feel better/worse.

If you find a link between certain activities and strong feelings, then try planning your time differently. Where possible, try and do more of those activities that make you feel good and less of those that make you feel bad.

Jane gets ready for school

Jane got up at 6.30 a.m. each day to go to school. She was dressed and ready to go by 7.15 a.m. and then sat around for the next 45 minutes. During this time, she would worry about school, her work, and what she would say to her friends. By 8.00 a.m., when it was time to leave home, she felt very worried and unhappy and often felt unable to go.

Once Jane had identified this pattern, she tried to arrange her morning routine differently. She got up later at 7.30 a.m. This meant that all her time before leaving for school was now taken up. She was busy and had less time to worry about what might happen.

At other times, when she woke up early, she got herself ready for school. Instead of sitting in a chair and worrying, she practised her musical instrument until it was time to leave the house. Jane found that her music helped her to feel relaxed. She was busy, she felt calm, and her mind was no longer playing tricks on her.

Mary returns home

Mary was always the first home from school and had one hour on her own before anyone else arrived. She kept a diary and discovered that this was the worst time of the day for her. She felt very scared of being on her own and thought horrible things would happen to her.

Mary decided to change her routine. Instead of coming straight home after school, she planned something different. She arranged to do the things she enjoyed. She visited her grandparents and went shopping with her friends. She now arrived home at the same time as the rest of her family feeling calmer and happier.

Helpful Tips

If there are particular times of the day when you feel unpleasant, then try to change what you do.

Small steps

Sometimes starting an activity might feel too large a step to tackle all in one go. At these times, it might be useful to break the task into smaller steps.

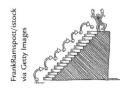
FrankRamspott/istock via Getty Images

▶ Each smaller step feels more manageable.

▶ This increases the chances of success, and each step will move you closer to your target.

Judy wants to swim

Judy liked swimming, but over the past six months, she had become down-hearted and unhappy and had not been swimming at all. She listed all of the activities that she wanted to start again, and chose swimming with her friend Susan as her number one choice.

Although she wanted to do it, the thought of going swimming with Susan seemed an enormous challenge. Judy decided to break this task down into smaller steps which she felt she could handle.

1. Go to the swimming pool and find out about opening times and cost.

2. Go on her own late one evening for a short 10-minute swim.

3. Go on her own one evening for a 30-minute swim.

4. Go swimming on her own one morning (when it is busier) for 30 minutes.

5. Go swimming with Susan one morning for 30 minutes.

Helpful Tips

Breaking large tasks into smaller steps can make them feel more manageable and help you to be successful.

Face you fears

Jslavy/Shutterstock

Breaking tasks into smaller steps is helpful, but you may still put off doing them because you **feel too anxious**.

Anxious feelings often stop us from doing the things we would really like to do.

However, by not doing them, we have to cope with other unpleasant feelings such as sadness and anger.

▶ You might feel very frightened about going to school, but staying at home may make you feel sad.

▶ You may feel scared about going out with your friends, but staying in on your own might make you feel angry.

At these times, it can be useful to **face your fears** and learn to overcome them. You can do this by using the following steps.

Step 1:   Use **small steps** to break down your challenge into smaller tasks.

Step 2:   Think about your **positive** and **coping self-talk** and practice using it.

Step 3:   **Relax and imagine** yourself successfully coping with your first task.

Step 4:   **Test it** out, one task at a time.

Step 5:   **Praise yourself** for being successful.

Kim is afraid to go out

Kim was afraid to go out of the house on her own ever since she was pushed over by a gang of boys. She was feeling very unhappy at being trapped in her house but was very scared of going out. She decided to **face her fears**.

Step 1: Kim decided that she would like to be able to go to the shop at the bottom of her road. By using **small steps**, she identified the following steps:

1. to stand by her front gate for a couple of minutes
2. to go outside the gate and then return home
3. to go out of the gate, walk to the bus stop, and then return home
4. to walk to the shops (not to go in them) and then return home
5. to walk to the shops and go in

Step 2: Kim thought about her **coping self-talk** as she prepared to go out. She practiced saying to herself, *'I am going to do this'; 'I am going to reclaim my life'*.

She practiced her **positive self-talk**. As she imagined herself walking to the gate she would say, *'I'm almost there. That was easier than I thought. I have done really well'*.

Step 3: Kim imagined her relaxing place. Once she was **relaxed, she imagined** a picture of herself coming out of the house and calmly walking to the front gate and then returning into her house.

Step 4: After imagining this a few times and practising her coping self-talk, Kim felt ready to **test it out**. Kim decided the best time to face her fears was during school-time when she would be less likely to meet any groups of children. She chose the time, relaxed herself, used her coping self-talk, and tested her first step.

Step 5: When she came in after being successful, Kim **praised and rewarded** herself with a mug of hot chocolate and a biscuit. She practiced this step a few times before moving on to the next step.

Helpful Tips

Don't let you fears take over and stop you from doing things. Take control and learn to overcome your fears.

Dump your habits

xpixel/Shutterstock

Sometimes our behaviour becomes a problem because there are things we can't stop doing. You may find that you are always

▶ **checking** – that doors are shut or that lights or taps are turned off.

▶ **cleaning** – perhaps your room or changing your clothes or washing your hands.

> **counting** – having to repeat things three or four times or doing things in a certain order.

Habits like these are often a way of switching off anxious or unpleasant feelings. These feelings are usually brought about by our thoughts. For example, we may **think** that if we

> don't constantly check, then something bad will happen.

> don't constantly clean, then we might catch germs and diseases or pass these on to others.

> don't count and do things in a certain order, then someone may be hurt.

The habits may make you feel better, but the relief they bring does not last. It will not be long before the thoughts and unpleasant feelings return, and the habits have to be repeated again and again and again.

Helpful Tips

When this happens, you need to **dump your habits** and prove that anxious feelings can be turned off **without** using your habits.

Step 1: Make a **habit ladder**. Write down all your habits on a piece of paper or on post-it notes. Now put them in order of difficulty. Put those that are most difficult to stop at the top of the ladder, and those that are easier to stop at the bottom.

Step 2: **Plan to be successful**.

> When will you try your first step?

> Plan how you will deal with your unpleasant feelings.

> What positive and coping self-talk will you use?

> Do you need someone to help you dump your habits?

Step 3: Try it, but this time **dump your habits** and see how long you can hold on without using them. When you start to hold on, use the **thermometer** from Chapter 12 to rate how your feel. Keep holding on, **dump your habits**, and keep rating you feelings. You will find that your worrying feelings will start to reduce!

Step 4: Remember to **praise yourself** for being successful

You will need to keep practicing. It may also be useful to involve someone else who can help to make sure that you don't use your habits. Once you have been successful, move on to the next step of your habit ladder.

Helpful Tips — Dump your habits and remember that your unpleasant feelings will come down without using your habits

David is worried about germs

David stood in some dog mess and became very worried about germs. He was always cleaning his shoes, and after he finished doing this, he would wash his hands over and over again. If he felt his hands were dirty, then he would have to clean anything he touched, including his clothes – which he changed three or four times each day. David had finally reached the stage where he wanted to **dump his habits**.

Step 1: David made a **habit ladder** and put his habits in order. He thought that the following would be the easiest to stop:

1 Delay changing his clothes after coming home from school for 30 minutes.
2 Only change his clothes once a day.
3 Limit his hand-washing, and each time wash his hands no more than twice.

The list went on until David reached the final stage of walking around the house in his shoes.

Step 2: David **planned to be successful**. He decided he would keep his mind busy by using **mind games** (puzzles), and he practiced his **coping self-talk**: *'I am in charge. I am not going to be bossed around by these habits anymore'*.

Step 3: David tried it. As soon as he felt the need to change his clothes, he tried to wait and **dump his habits**. He used the **thermometer** to rate his fear and gave himself a rating of 8. After five minutes, his feelings had got worse and had gone up to number 9. He held on, used his **coping self-talk** and tried to relax. After 15 minutes, the feelings didn't seem so strong, and his fear rating was now down to 5. He held out for 30 minutes and then changed his clothes.

Step 4: David was really **pleased with himself** and treated himself to a special DVD.

The next time he tried this he held out for over an hour. The feelings seemed to become weaker even though he didn't use his habits.

Remember to reward yourself

It is important to remember to reward yourself for trying to change what you do. You are trying to take some big steps to

▶ reclaim your life

▶ keep yourself well

▶ change the way you think

▶ manage your emotions

▶ behave differently

You should be proud of what you are trying to do, so think about how you can reward yourself. It doesn't matter whether you were successful or not – you are trying and that is what is important.

Rewards don't have to cost lots of money. They are a way of you showing yourself that you **notice, acknowledge, and celebrate** what you have done. Rewards could be

▶ Saying to yourself 'well done', 'good job', or telling someone special what you have achieved.

▶ Spending extra time doing something you enjoy like playing video games or going for a cycle.

▶ Celebrating with a special treat like watching an episode of your favourite box set, making yourself a hot chocolate, or having biscuit or slice of cake.

▶ Treating yourself to a special activity like a long bath with candles, painting your nails, buying something you have wanted.

▶ Arrange to hang out with a friend, have a sleepover, or go somewhere special.

Whatever you decide celebrate and acknowledge that you are trying to help yourself.

davib/Shutterstock

Remember!

Activity can help you to feel better and gives you less time to listen to your negative thoughts.

If there are times of the day or week that are difficult, plan your timetable differently.

Break your challenges into smaller steps. This will help you to be successful.

Face you fears and learn to overcome your difficulties.

If you have problems checking, cleaning, or counting, learn to dump your habits.

Keep practicing and reward yourself when you have tried to help yourself.

Activity diary

Keep a diary each day of what you have done and how you have felt. Use the Thermometer from Chapter 12 to rate the strength of these feelings.

What you did Activity	How you felt Feelings
7.00 Morning	
8.00	
9.00	
10.00	
11.00	
12.00	
1.00 Afternoon	
2.00	
3.00	
4.00	
5.00	
6.00	
7.00	
8.00	
9.00	
10.00	
11.00	
12.00	

Is there any pattern linking what you do and how you feel?

Things that make me feel good

Write or draw the places, activities or people that make you feel good

Things that makes me feel unpleasant

Write or draw the places, activities, or people that make you feel unpleasant.

Have more fun

When we feel unpleasant, we stop doing things, even the things we enjoy.
Write down the activities you enjoy in the boxes below.

Activities I enjoy but have stopped doing

Activities I like but don't do very often

Activities I would like to do

**Which of these would you like to do to help you get busier and to
reclaim your life?**

Small steps

Sometimes tasks or challenges seem too big. When this happens, we need to break them down into smaller steps. This will make each step more possible and will help you to be successful.

Write what you want to and the smaller steps that will take you towards your goal.

My goal – what I want to do

Break your goal into smaller steps and write or draw them here

Arrange your steps in order of difficulty. Put the hardest at the top (1) and the easiest at the bottom (5).

1.

2.

3.

4.

5.

Start with the easiest step. Once you have been successful, move on to the next.

Habit ladder

If you have lots of habits, write them down on a habit ladder.

Write down all of your habits and then put them in order of difficulty. Put those that are most difficult to stop at the top of the ladder, and those that are easier to stop at the bottom.

> My Habits

Hardest to stop

Easiest to stop

Start with the easiest and then climb the ladder to boss back your habit.

Face your fears

My goal – what I want to do

Step 1. Use **small steps** to break your goal into easier steps.

My steps to success are

Step 2. What is your **coping self-talk**?

Step 3. **Relax and imagine** yourself being successful. Repeat your coping self-talk as you imagine successfully achieving your first step. Practice this a few times.

Step 4. Choose a time when you will face your fear, relax, and **test it out**.

Remember to use your coping self-talk.

Step 5. **Praise and reward** yourself for facing your fear.

You may want to practice each step a few times, but once you feel confident move on to the next one and repeat each step until you have overcome your fear.

Dump your habits

Use these four steps to gain control of your life and to dump your habits.

Step 1. Use the **habit ladder**. Write down all of your habits and put them in order of difficulty.

Start with the easier habits, and write down below the habit you are going to dump.

Step 2. **Plan to be successful**. Write down

▶ When will you try your first step?

▶ How you will deal with your unpleasant feelings and keep calm.

▶ What is your positive and coping self-talk?

▶ Do you need someone to help you dump your habits? Who can help you?

Step 3. Try it and **dump your habit**. Use the Thermometer from Chapter 12 and keep rating how you are feeling.

Step 4. **Praise and reward yourself** for dumping your habit.

Once you have been successful move up to the next step of your habit ladder and dump the next habit.

Reward yourself

It is important to reward yourself. You are trying to help yourself by facing your challenges, and you need to celebrate what you are trying to do.

Write down in the boxes below some of the things you can do to reward yourself.

> What can I say to myself or who I can tell?

> Can I reward myself with extra time doing something I enjoy?

> What special treats can I reward myself with?

> What activities could I do to celebrate?

> What could I do with other people to reward myself?

Learning to solve problems

Each day brings a new set of problems and challenges. For example

▷ dealing with being unfairly being told off by a teacher

▷ trying to stay in your seat at school

▷ coping with teasing by an annoying brother or sister

▷ negotiating with your parents to stay up late

When we encounter a problem, we have to think about the different ways we could deal with it and then make a decision about what we will do or say.

Sometimes we make the right choice, while at other times, we seem to get it wrong. There will always be times when this happens, but some people seem to make more wrong choices or find it harder to solve problems than others. When this happens, it is useful to think about how you are dealing with your problems and whether you could try to solve them in different ways.

Why do problems happen?

There are many reasons why we are unable to successfully solve our problems. Three of these reasons are particularly common.

Acting without thinking

Decisions and choices are sometimes made too quickly. You may rush into something without really thinking through what will happen.

> Nick heard his dad say that he had left the shopping in the car. Wanting to be helpful, Nick rushed out and carried all the bags from the backseat of the car into the house. Nick didn't check with his parents, but if he had he would have found out that their shopping was in the car boot. The bags he bought in were for a party his dad was organising at work.

> Sabrina heard her teacher's instructions to copy her work into her book, and she immediately picked up her pen and started. Unfortunately, she didn't hear the next instruction, which told her to use a pencil and to start her work on a new page.

Nick and Sabrina were both trying to be helpful, but in their rush, they created more problems for themselves.

Feelings take over

Scc.comics/Shutterstock

Strong feelings like anger or anxiety sometimes take over and stop us from thinking problems through and making choices about what we do or say.

> Mike became very angry when he was tackled during a game of football and kicked the other player. The referee sent Mike off the pitch.

> Jenny didn't understand her schoolwork but was really worried about asking her teacher for help. She didn't ask, she got her homework wrong, and she had to stay behind after school and do it again.

Mike knew that if he kicked someone, he would be sent off. Jenny knew that if she got her work wrong, she would have to do it again. At the time, Mike and Jenny were not able to think about the consequences of their behaviour. Strong feelings took over and prevented them from thinking these situations through.

Can't see any other solution

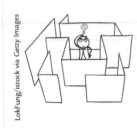

LokFung/istock via Getty Images

The third main reason why we can't solve problems is because we just can't think of another way of doing things. We become fixed in our ideas and can't see any other solutions.

Lightspring/Shutterstock

Helpful Tips

We need to find some new ways to solve our problems so that we can make more successful choices.

Learn to stop and think

It is useful to learn a way of dealing with problems which ensures that you don't rush in with the first thing that comes into your head. A helpful way is to use the **Stop, Plan, and Go** traffic-light system

serhio/Shutterstock

▶ *RED*. Before you do anything, think of the red traffic light and **Stop**.

▶ *AMBER*. **Plan** and think about what you want to do or say.

▶ *GREEN*. **Go** with your plan.

The first step is often the hardest, and sometimes, you may find it hard to **STOP** yourself from rushing in. Practice imagining a picture of some traffic lights and as you see the red light, think to yourself **STOP**. As the light comes on, take a few deep breaths. This may help you to calm and slow down enough to let you plan and think about what you want to do. The more you practice, the easier it will become.

You can also use this system at school. You can remind yourself by putting red, amber, and green coloured strips around a pencil or ruler or on you pencil case. Seeing the strips will help you to think, '**Stop, Plan, and Go**', but no one else will know what the strips mean.

Helpful Tips

Stop, plan, and go can be a helpful way of dealing with problems if you tend to rush in without thinking.

Identify different solutions

Sometimes we meet the same problem and challenge every day but often end up making the wrong decision time and time again. When this happens, it is useful to stop and think about all the different ways in which you can deal with this problem.

Take a sheet of paper and write down all the possible solutions you can think of in two minutes. The idea is to get as many ideas as you can, so don't worry if some of them seem unrealistic or silly.

Another way of doing this is to use the '**OR**' method. Keep asking yourself 'OR' to find as many possible solutions as you can.

Billy is ignored

Billy felt that his friends often ignored him, so he used the '**OR**' method to find ways in which he could get his friends to listen to him:

▶ I could talk louder **OR**

▶ shout **OR**

▶ stand in front of their faces so that they would have to listen to me **OR**

▶ keep repeating myself **OR**

▶ talk with one person rather than all the group **OR**

▶ find things to talk about that really interested them **OR**

▶ find a new group of friends

For Billy, the idea of shouting all the time seemed silly, and changing his group of friends was not really possible. Some of the other ideas, he came up with were more useful.

Billy decided that he needed to listen more carefully to the things that really interested his friends. He also decided that he would try to talk more with people on their own, rather than trying to join in with the group discussions.

If you find it hard to think of any different ways of dealing with your problems, then it may be useful to talk it over with someone else. Ask how they would deal with your problem, and see if they can suggest some different ideas.

Helpful Tips

Try using the OR method to identify different ways you could deal with your problems.

Think through the consequences

Once you have made a list of possible solutions, the next step is to work out which is the best one. Think about the positive and negative consequences of each idea and then choose the one that you think, on balance, will work best. This involves five steps.

1 What is my problem?

2 How could I deal with this problem?

3 What are the positive consequences of each solution?

4 What are the negative consequences of each solution?

5 On balance, what is the best solution?

Marla Gets Teased

Three girls at school have started to tease Marla and call her names at break time. On the first day, Marla became very angry and chased after the girls. On the second day, she hit one of the girls and ended up in trouble with the head teacher. On the third day, she called the girls names back, but this seemed to make the name-calling worse. Marla decided to sit down and work out how she would cope with this problem.

My Problem: Being teased by Emma, Kate, and Jo		
What I could do	**Positive consequences**	**Negative consequences**
Hit them whenever they called me names OR	*Would make me feel better!*	*I'd get into more trouble. I might be suspended from school. They may start to hit me.*
Find a teacher to tell OR	*The teacher would sort it out, and I wouldn't get into any more trouble.*	*They may tease me even more for telling the teacher. I may not be able to find a teacher.*
Ignore them OR	*If I don't react they might get bored.*	*BUT I CAN'TDO IT because they annoy me so much!*
Stay away from them at break times	*They can't tease me. I won't get into trouble. They might find something else to do.*	*This might not always be easy. They might come and look for me.*

On balance, the best way to solve this problem is to stay out of their way at breaktimes. If they come and find me, I'll move away and move closer to a teacher.

Thinking this problem through was helpful for Marla. Although hitting the girls made her feel better, she also realised that this had other consequences which were not good. Marla weighed up all the ideas, and on balance, she chose to stay away from the girls at breaktimes.

> **Helpful Tips**
>
> Thinking through the short- and long-term consequences for you and others can help you to choose the best solution.

Remind yourself what to do

Christophe BOISSON/Shutterstock

There will be times when although you know the best way of dealing with your problems, you slip back into your old ways as your new plans are **forgotten**.

If this happens, you need to work out how you can remind yourself to use your new plan.

Michael fiddles with his pencil case

Michael was in trouble every day at school for fiddling with his pencils and pencil case. He wanted to stop this habit, and he problem-solved with his teacher about what he could do. He decided that he might be able to stop fiddling by sitting on his hands when the teacher was speaking. He agreed with his teacher that she would lightly touch his shoulder if Michael forgot. Michael also decided to put his pencil case in his bag, rather than leaving it out on his desk. Michael stuck a sign on the inside of his pencil case saying, 'Put me in your bag', to help him remember.

Jemma's room is always untidy

Jemma was always in trouble at home for having an untidy bedroom. This became more of a problem for her recently since her parents had stopped her pocket money. Even when she tried to tidy her room, she never seemed to get it right. There was always something she forgot to do. She decided that she had to stop this happening, and she drew up a 'tidy bedroom checklist' which she put on her bedroom wall. She listed all the things she needed to do to tidy her room:

Dmitry Natashin/
Shutterstock

> Pick clothes up off the floor.

> Put dirty clothes in the washing bin.

- Put clean clothes in drawers and wardrobe.

- Make bed.

- Put magazines and books in a tidy pile.

- Put CD's in their cases.

Jemma agreed with her parents when she would tidy her room, and she used the list to make sure that she did not forget to do anything.

Henry gets wound up

Henry has a very quick temper and became very angry – shouting, swearing, and sometimes hitting out. He was always fighting and had recently been suspended from school for two days.

Henry problem-solved this with his best friend and decided that he needed to 'bail-out' of arguments. He needed to stop and walk away rather than stay and argue. This was not easy for Henry, so his friend agreed that he would help. When Henry started to become angry, his friend would tell him to 'bail out'. This was the signal for Henry to stop, walk away, and calm down. Henry's friend was very helpful and, although not easy, Henry started to learn that he could deal with arguments in a better way.

Helpful Tips

Find ways to remind yourself to use your new ideas when you need them.

Practice getting it right

iqoncept/123RF

Learning to deal with problems in new or different ways is not always easy. It can take time, and you may need to practice before you get it right. As with most things, the more you practice, the easier it will become.

Imagine yourself changing the ending

Think about your problem and imagine yourself solving it differently. Instead of using your old solutions, **change the ending**, and imagine yourself being successful.

Choose a quiet time and get a really good picture of your problem situation in your mind.

> Describe the scene as well as you can.

> Imagine who will be there.

> Think about what is going on and what is being said.

> imagine yourself using your new solution and being successful.

> Remember to praise yourself for solving your problem.

Millie rushes around

Millie was always in trouble at school for rushing around. Sometimes she would knock and push people in her hurry to be first. Millie decided that she needed to calm down, and that she would count to five before she did anything.

Millie imagined herself using this idea at the end of lessons, going into the dining hall, and coming in after lunchtime. Imagining herself counting and becoming calm helped her prepare to use this idea when she got to school.

Practice acting it out

dedMazay/Shutterstock

It is useful to practice using your new skills by acting out your problem situations with friends. Try to make the situation as real as possible, and think about who will be there, what will be said, and how they will react. Try out different solutions and see what works well.

Acting out problem situations can be good fun, and if you take it in turns, you may find that you can learn some useful tips from your friends!

Helpful Tips

Practicing being successful will help you to use your new ideas when you need them.

Plan to be successful

Problem solving is often used to **stop things happening**:

> Marla wanted to stop being teased.

> Michael wanted his teacher to stop telling him off.

> Henry wanted to stop fighting.

Another way to solve problems is to think about the things you want to happen and then **plan how you can be successful**.

Kia wants to sleepover

Kia wanted to sleep at her friend's house, but she didn't think her mum would let her. They were having lots of arguments, and Kia knew that unless this changed her mum would not allow a sleepover.

Kia problem-solved how this could change. She knew this would take time, and she saw the main job as stopping the arguments with her mum. Most of these were about Kia not helping around the house, so she decided that she would start to keep her room tidy. She also decided that she would help to lay the table for meals and help with washing up afterwards. Kia's mother was very surprised and also very pleased. They argued less, and after a week, Kia asked her mother if she could sleep at her friends. Her mother agreed saying that if Kia was now prepared to help around the house, then she should be allowed some special privileges.

Talk yourself through it

Another useful way of learning to solve problems is to ask someone who is successful to talk you through what they do.

▶ Ask them to tell you what they do.

▶ Watch them doing it.

▶ Then talk yourself through your problem.

This can be very helpful for those problems that seem to occur fairly often.

Mike doesn't know what to say to his friends

Mike felt very worried when he met his friends because he often did not know what to talk about. His friend Reuben was very popular and always seemed to know what to say, so Mike asked for his help.

Reuben said that when he arrived at school each morning, he would go up to his group of friends, say hello and talk about something that had been on television last night, such as a sports match or the latest episode of their favourite TV soap. Reuben went to school with Mike the next day and as they arrived Reuben talked out aloud what he was going to do as Mike watched.

The next day, when Mike arrived at school, he talked out aloud what he was going to do. 'I'm going to walk across the playground, go up to Max and Errol, say hello, and ask if they saw what happened on our favourite TV soap last night'. Mike did this and was pleased to find that he was soon chatting with his friends. The next day he talked himself through it again, and after a few times, Mike found that he was now doing this without thinking.

davib/Shutterstock

Remember!

- Don't rush – learn to **STOP, PLAN, and GO**.

- Think about the **different ways** in which you could solve your problem.

- Think through the **consequences** of each solution.

- On **balance** choose the best solution.

- Ask someone successful to tell you what they do, then watch them and finally **talk yourself through it**.

- Find ways to **remind** yourself to use your plans.

Identify possible solutions – 'OR'

What is my problem?

Now write down **ALL** the possible ways in which you can solve this problem. The idea is to find as many different solutions as possible.

1. I could solve this problem by

2. **OR**

3. **OR**

4. **OR**

5. **OR**

6. **OR**

7. **OR**

Ask someone who is successful

It is useful to find out how other people might solve this problem.

Think of someone who could help, and ask them what ideas they might suggest.

I asked:

They suggested I could solve this problem by:

What are the consequences?

Write down your problem and list the different solutions you have identified. Think about the negative and positive consequences of each solution and write these down. When you have finished, look at your list, and on balance, choose the best solution for your problem.

My Problem:		
What I could do	**Positive consequences**	**Negative consequences**
1.		
2.		
3.		
4.		
5.		
6.		
On balance, the best way to solve this problem is		

Looking for solutions

Write or draw your problem and fill out all the possible solutions you can think of

My Problem

Talk yourself through it

If you find that the same problem occurs over and over again, then find out how someone else copes, watch them do it, and then talk yourself through their plan for success.

What is my problem?

Who could I talk with who is successful?

How do they deal with this problem?

When can I watch them talk me through their plan?

When will I use this plan, and what will I say to myself?

How am I going to reward myself for being successful?

How did it go?

Stop, plan, and go

Use the traffic lights to help you to plan how you will deal with your problem.

STOP. What is your problem?

PLAN. What is your solution?

GO. When will you try it out?

References

Barrett, P. (2004). *Friends for Life: Group Leaders Manual for Children*. Bowen Hills: Australian Academic Press.

Barrett, P., Webster, H., and Turner, C. (2000). *FRIENDS Prevention of Anxiety and Depression for Children. Children's Workbook*. Australia: Australian Academic Press.

Beck, A.T. (1976). *Cognitive Therapy and the Emotional Disorders*. New York: International Universities Press.

Beck, A.T., Rush, A.J., Shaw, B.F., and Emery, G. (1979). *Cognitive Therapy of Depression*. New York: Guilford press.

Belsher, G. and Wilkes, T.C.R. (1994). Ten key principles of adolescent cognitive therapy. In: *Cognitive Therapy for Depressed Adolescents* (eds. T.C.R. Wilkes, G. Belsher, A.J. Rush and E. Frank). New York: Guilford Press.

Boydell, K.M., Hodgins, M., Pignatiello, A. et al. (2014). Using technology to deliver mental health services to children and youth: a scoping review. *Journal of the Canadian Academy of Child and Adolescent Psychiatry* 23(2): 87–99.

Breinholst, S., Esbjørn, B.H., Reinholdt-Dunne, M.L., and Stallard, P. (2012). CBT for the treatment of child anxiety disorders: a review of why parental involvement has not enhanced outcomes. *Journal of Anxiety Disorders* 26(3): 416–424.

Burns, D.D. (1980). *Feeling Good: The New Mood Therapy*. New York: New American Library.

Calear, A.L. and Christensen, H. (2010). Systematic review of school-based prevention and early intervention programs for depression. *Journal of Adolescence* 33(3): 429–438.

Cary, C.E. and McMillen, J.C. (2012). The data behind the dissemination: a systematic review of trauma-focused cognitive behavioral therapy for use with children and youth. *Children and Youth Services Review* 34(4): 748–757.

Chorpita, B.F., Daleiden, E.L., Ebesutani, C. et al. (2011). Evidence-based treatments for children and adolescents: an updated review of indicators of efficacy and effectiveness. *Clinical Psychology: Science and Practice* 18(2): 154–172.

Dodge, K.A. (1985). Attributional bias in aggressive children. In: *Advances in Cognitive-Behavioural Research and Therapy*, vol. 4 (ed. P.C. Kendall). New York: Academic Press.

Doherr, E.A., Corner, J.M., and Evans, E. (1999). *Pilot Study of Young Children's Abilities to Use the Concepts Central to Cognitive Behavioural Therapy*. Norwich: University of East Anglia.

Doherr, L., Reynolds, S., Wetherly, J., and Evans, E.H. (2005). Young children's ability to engage in cognitive therapy tasks: associations with age and educational experience. *Behavioural and Cognitive Psychotherapy* 33(02): 201–215.

Donnelly, K.C. (2012). *Starving the Anger Gremlin: A Cognitive Behaviour Workbook in Anger Management for Young People*. London: Jessica Kingsley.

Donnelly, K.C. (2013). *Starving the Anxiety Gremlin: A Cognitive Behaviour Workbook on Anxiety Management for Young People*. London: Jessica Kingsley.

Ellis, A. (1962). *Reason and Emotion in Psychotherapy*. New York: Lyle-Stewart.

Fisher, E., Heathcote, L., Palermo, T.M. et al. (2014). Systematic review and meta-analysis of psychological therapies for children with chronic pain. *Journal of Pediatric Psychology* 39(8): 763–782.

Flavell, J.H., Flavell, E.R., and Green, F.L. (2001). Development of children's understanding of connections between thinking and feeling. *Psychological Science* 12: 430–432.

Fonagy, P., Cottrell, D., Phillips, J. et al. (2014). *What Works for Whom?: A Critical Review of Treatments for Children and Adolescents*. Guilford Publications.

Franklin, M.E., Kratz, H.E., Freeman, J.B. et al. (2015). Cognitive-Behavioral Therapy for Pediatric Obsessive-Compulsive Disorder: Empirical Review and Clinical Recommendations. *Psychiatry Research* 227(1): 78–92.

Freeman, J.B., Garcia, A.M., Coyne, L. et al. (2008). Early childhood OCD: Preliminary findings from a family-based cognitive-behavioral approach. *Journal of the American Academy of Child & Adolescent Psychiatry* 47(5): 593–602.

Friedberg, R.D. and McClure, J.M. (2015). *Clinical Practice of Cognitive Therapy with Children and Adolescents: The Nuts and Bolts*. Guilford Publications.

Friedberg, R.D. and Wilt, L.H. (2010). Metaphors and stories in cognitive behavioral therapy with children. *Journal of Rational-Emotive & Cognitive-Behavior Therapy* 28(2): 100–113.

Gilbert, P. (2009). Introducing compassion-focused therapy. *Advances in Psychiatric Treatment* 15(3): 199–208.

Gilbert, P. (2014). The origins and nature of compassion focused therapy. *British Journal of Clinical Psychology* 53(1): 6–41.

Gillies, D., Taylor, F., Gray, C. et al. (2013). Psychological therapies for the treatment of post-traumatic stress disorder in children and adolescents (Review). *Evidence-Based Child Health: A Cochrane Review Journal* 8(3): 1004–1116.

Grave, J. and Blissett, J. (2004). Is cognitive behavior therapy developmentally appropriate for young children? A critical review of the evidence. *Clinical Psychology Review* 24(4): 399–420.

Greenberger, D. and Padesky, C.A. (1995). *Mind Over Mood*. New York: Guilford.

Harrington, R., Wood, A., and Verduyn, C. (1998). Clinically depressed adolescents. In: *Cognitive Behaviour Therapy for Children and Families* (ed. P. Graham). Cambridge: Cambridge University Press.

Hayes, S.C. (2004). Acceptance and commitment therapy, relational frame theory, and the third wave of behavioral and cognitive therapies. *Behavior Therapy* 35(4): 639–665.

Hayes, S.C., Luoma, J.B., Bond, F.W. et al. (2006). Acceptance and commitment therapy: model, processes and outcomes. *Behaviour Research and Therapy* 44(1): 1–25.

Hetrick, S.E., Cox, G.R., Witt, K.G. et al. (2016). Cognitive behavioural therapy (CBT), third-wave CBT and interpersonal therapy (IPT) based interventions for preventing depression in children and adolescents. *The Cochrane Library* doi: 10.1002/14651858.CD003380.pub4.

Hirshfeld-Becker, D.R., Masek, B., Henin, A. et al. (2008). Cognitive-behavioral intervention with young anxious children. *Harvard Review of Psychiatry* 16(2): 113–125.

Hirshfeld-Becker, D.R., Masek, B., Henin, A. et al. (2010). Cognitive behavioral therapy for 4-to 7-year-old children with anxiety disorders: a randomized clinical trial. *Journal of Consulting and Clinical Psychology* 78(4): 498.

Hofmann, S.G., Sawyer, A.T., and Fang, A. (2010). The empirical status of the "new wave" of cognitive behavioral therapy. *Psychiatric Clinics of North America* 33(3): 701–710.

Hughes, J.N. (1988). *Cognitive Behaviour Therapy with Children in Schools*. New York: Pergamon Press.

Ironside, V. and Rodgers, F. (2011). *The Huge Bag of Worries*. London: Hodder Children's Books.

Jackson, H.J. and King, N.J. (1981). The emotive imagery treatment of a child's trauma-induced phobia. *Journal of Behavior Therapy and Experimental Psychiatry* 12(4): 325–328.

James, A.C., James, G., Cowdrey, F.A. et al. (2013). Cognitive behavioural therapy for anxiety disorders in children and adolescents. *Cochrane Database of Systematic Reviews* 6.

Kane, M.T. and Kendall, P.C. (1989). Anxiety disorders in children: a multiple-baseline evaluation of a cognitive-behavioral treatment. *Behavior Therapy* 20(4): 499–508.

Kendall, P.C. (1992). *Coping Cat Program for Anxious Youth*. Ardmore, PA: Workbook Publishing.

Kendall, P.C. and Chansky, T.E. (1991). Considering cognition in anxiety-disordered children. *Journal of Anxiety Disorders* 5(2): 167–185.

Kendall, P.C. and Hollon, S.D. (1979). *Cognitive-Behavioural Interventions: Overview and Current Status. Cognitive-Behavioural Intervention: Theory Research and Procedures*. New York: Academic Press.

Kendall, P.C. and Panichelli-Mindel, S.M. (1995). Cognitive-behavioral treatments. *Journal of Abnormal Child Psychology* 23(1): 107–124.

Kendall, P.C., Stark, K.D., and Adam, T. (1990). Cognitive deficit or cognitive distortion in childhood depression. *Journal of Abnormal Child Psychology* 18(3): 255–270.

Killick, S., Curry, V., and Myles, P. (2016). The mighty metaphor: a collection of therapists' favourite metaphors and analogies. *The Cognitive Behaviour Therapist* 9: doi: 10.1017/S1754470X16000210.

Klaus Minde, M.D., Rhona Bezonsky, M.S.W., and BA, A.H. (2010). The effectiveness of CBT in 3–7 year old anxious children: preliminary data. *Journal of the Canadian Academy of Child and Adolescent Psychiatry* 19: 109.

Leitenberg, H., Yost, L.W., and Carroll-Wilson, M. (1986). Negative cognitive errors in children: questionnaire development, normative data, and comparisons between children with and without self-reported symptoms of depression, low self-esteem, and evaluation anxiety. *Journal of Consulting and Clinical Psychology* 54(4): 528.

Lochman, J.E., White, K.J., and Wayland, K.K. (1991). Cognitive behavioral assessments and treatment with aggressive children. In: *Therapy with Children and Adolescents: Cognitive Behavioral Procedures* (ed. P. Kendall). New York: Guildford Press.

March, J.S., Mulle, K., and Herbel, B. (1994). Behavioural psychotherapy for children and adolescents with obsessive-compulsive disorder: an open clinical trial of a new protocol driven treatment package. *Journal of the American Academy of Child and Adolescent Psychiatry* 33: 333–341.

Miller, W.R. and Rollnick, S. (1991). *Motivational Interviewing*. New York, NY: Guilford Press.

Monga, S., Young, A., and Owens, M. (2009). Evaluating a cognitive behavioral therapy group program for anxious five to seven year old children: a pilot study. *Depression and Anxiety* 26(3): 243–250.

Muris, P. and Field, A.P. (2008). Distorted cognition and pathological anxiety in children and adolescents. *Cognition and Emotion* 22(3): 395–421.

Neil, A.L. and Christensen, H. (2009). Efficacy and effectiveness of school-based prevention and early intervention programs for anxiety. *Clinical Psychology Review* 29(3): 208–215.

de Oliveiraa, I.R., Matosb, A.C., Ribeiroc, M.G., and Velasquezb, M.L. (2015). Changing adolescent dysfunctional core beliefs with group trial-based cognitive training (G-TBCT): proposal of a preventative approach in schools. *Current Psychiatry Reviews* 11: 1–14.

Palermo, T.M., Eccleston, C., Lewandowski, A.S. et al. (2010). Randomized controlled trials of psychological therapies for management of chronic pain in children and adolescents: an updated meta-analytic review. *Pain* 148(3): 387–397.

Pavlov, I. (1927). *Conditioning Reflexes*. Oxford: Oxford University Press.

Perry, D.G., Perry, L.C., and Rasmussen, P. (1986). Cognitive social learning mediators of aggression. *Child Development* 57(3): 700–711.

Phillips, N. (1999). *The Panic Book*. Australia: Shrink-Rap Press.

Quakley, S., Reynolds, S., and Coker, S. (2004). The effects of cues on young children's abilities to discriminate among thoughts, feelings and behaviours. *Behaviour Research and Therapy* 42: 343–356.

Rehm, L.P. and Carter, A.S. (1990). Cognitive components of depression. In: *Handbook of developmental psychopathology* (eds. M. Lewis and S.M. Miller), 341–351. Springer US.

Reynolds, S., Wilson, C., Austin, J., and Hooper, L. (2012). Effects of psychotherapy for anxiety in children and adolescents: a meta-analytic review. *Clinical Psychology Review* 32(4): 251–262.

Rolfsnes, E.S. and Idsoe, T. (2011). School-based intervention programs for PTSD symptoms: a review and meta-analysis. *Journal of Traumatic Stress* 24(2): 155–165.

Ronen, T. (1992). Cognitive therapy with young children. *Child Psychiatry and Human Development* 23(1): 19–30.

Rosenstiel, A.K. and Scott, D.S. (1977). Four considerations in using imagery techniques with children. *Journal of Behavior Therapy and Experimental Psychiatry* 8(3): 287–290.

Scheeringa, M.S., Weems, C.F., Cohen, J.A. et al. (2011). Trauma-focused cognitive-behavioral therapy for posttraumatic stress disorder in three-through six year-old children: a randomized clinical trial. *Journal of Child Psychology and Psychiatry* 52(8): 853–860.

Schniering, C.A. and Rapee, R.M. (2004). The relationship between automatic thoughts and negative emotions in children and adolescents: a test of the cognitive content-specificity hypothesis. *Journal of Abnormal Psychology* 113(3): 464.

Segal, Z.V., Williams, J.M.G., and Teasdale, J.D. (2012). *Mindfulness-Based Cognitive Therapy for Depression*. Guilford Press.

Shafran, R., Fonagy, P., Pugh, K., and Myles, P. (2014). Transformation of mental health services for children and young people in England. In: *Dissemination and Implementation of Evidence-Based Practices in Child and Adolescent Mental Health*, vol. 158 (eds. R.S. Beidas and P.C. Kendall). New York, NY: Oxford University Press.

Skinner, B.F. (1974). *About Behaviorism*. London: Cape.

Spence, S.H., Donovan, C., and Brechman-Toussaint, M. (2000). The treatment of childhood social phobia: the effectiveness of a social; skills training based, cognitive-behavioural intervention, with and without parental involvement. *Journal of Child Psychology and Psychiatry* 41(6): 713–726.

Stallard, P. (2002). *Think Good Feel Good. A Cognitive Behaviour Therapy Workbook for Children and Young People*. Chichester: Wiley.

Stallard, P. (2005). *A Clinician's Guide to Think Good-Feel Good: Using CBT with Children and Young People*. Wiley.

Stallard, P., Skryabina, E., Taylor, G. et al. (2014). Classroom-based cognitive behaviour therapy (FRIENDS): a cluster randomised controlled trial to Prevent Anxiety in Children through Education in Schools (PACES). *The Lancet Psychiatry* 1(3): 185–192.

Stockings, E.A., Degenhardt, L., Dobbins, T. et al. (2016). Preventing depression and anxiety in young people: a review of the joint efficacy of universal, selective and indicated prevention. *Psychological Medicine* 46(01): 11–26.

Sunderland, M. (1997). *Draw on Your Emotions*. London: Routledge.

Sunderland, M. (2001). *A Nifflenoo Called Nevermind: A Story for Children Who Bottle Up Their Feelings*. London: Routledge.

Thapar, A., Collishaw, S., Pine, D.S., and Thapar, A.K. (2012). Depression in adolescence. *The Lancet* 379(9820): 1056–1067.

Turk, J. (1998). Children with learning difficulties and their parents. In: *Cognitive—Behaviour Therapy for Children and Families* (ed. P. Graham), 110–125. Cambridge UK: Cambridge University Press.

Verduyn, C. (2000). Cognitive behaviour therapy in childhood depression. *Child and Adolescent Mental Health* 5(4): 176–180.

Wellman, H.M., Hollander, M., and Schult, C.A. (1996). Young children's understanding of thought bubbles and thoughts. *Child Development* 67: 768–788.

Werner-Seidler, A., Perry, Y., Calear, A.L. et al. (2017). School-based depression and anxiety prevention programs for young people: a systematic review and meta-analysis. *Clinical Psychology Review* 51: 30–47.

Wever, C. (1999). *The School Wobblies*. Australia: Shrink-Rap Press.

Wever, C. (2000). *The Secret Problem*. Australia: Shrink-Rap Press.

Whitaker, S. (2001). Anger control for people with learning disabilities: a critical review. *Behavioural and Cognitive Psychotherapy* 29(03): 277–293.

Wolpe, J. (1958). *Reciprocal Inhibition Therapy*. Standford, CA: Stanford University Press.

Young, J. and Brown, P.F. (1996). Cognitive behaviour therapy for anxiety; practical tops for using it with children. *Clinical Psychology Forum* 91: 19–21.

Zhou, X., Hetrick, S.E., Cuijpers, P. et al. (2015). Comparative efficacy and acceptability of psychotherapies for depression in children and adolescents: a systematic review and network meta-analysis. *World Psychiatry* 14(2): 207–222.

Index

Think Good, Feel Good: A Cognitive Behavioural Therapy Workbook for Children and Young People, Second Edition. Paul Stallard.
© 2019 John Wiley & Sons Ltd. Published 2019 by John Wiley & Sons Ltd.
Companion website: www.wiley.com/go/thinkgoodfeelgood2e